THE ARAB HORSE, THE THOROUGHBRED, AND THE TURF

BY THE

HON. SIR JAMES PENN BOUCAUT, K.C.M.G.,
FORMERLY SENIOR PUISNE JUDGE OF THE SUPREME COURT OF
SOUTH AUSTRALIA, AND THREE TIMES PRIME
MINISTER OF THAT STATE

WITH A FOREWORD BY THE

RT. HON. SIR GEORGE H. REID, G.C.M.G.,
HIGH COMMISSIONER FOR AUSTRALIA

1912

Copyright © 2013 Read Books Ltd.
This book is copyright and may not be
reproduced or copied in any way without
the express permission of the publisher in writing

British Library Cataloguing-in-Publication Data
A catalogue record for this book is available from the
British Library

Horses – Breeding and Anatomy

The horse (*Equus ferus caballus*) is one of two extant subspecies of *Equus ferus*. It is an odd-toed ungulate mammal belonging to the taxonomic family 'Equidae'. The horse has evolved over the past 45 to 55 million years from a small multi-toed creature into the large, single-toed animal of today. Humans began to domesticate horses around 4000 BC, and their domestication is believed to have been widespread by 3000 BC. We, as humans have interacted with horses in a multitude of ways throughout history – from sport competitions and non-competitive recreational pursuits, to working activities such as police work, agriculture, entertainment and therapy. Horses have also been used in warfare, from which a wide variety of riding and driving techniques developed, using many different styles of equipment and methods of control. With this range of uses in mind, there is an equally extensive, specialized vocabulary used to describe equine-related concepts, covering everything from anatomy to life stages, size, colours, markings, breeds, locomotion, and behaviour. Horse anatomy is a fascinating topic, and in the course of this introduction, the basics will be discussed.

To start; the horse skeleton averages 250 bones. A significant difference between the horse skeleton and that of a human is the lack of a collarbone—the horse's forelimbs are attached to the spinal column by a powerful set of muscles, tendons, and ligaments that attach the shoulder blade to the torso. The horse's legs and hooves are also unique structures. Their leg bones are proportioned differently from those of a human. For example, the body part that is called a horse's 'knee' is actually made up of the carpal bones that correspond to the human wrist. Similarly, the hock contains bones equivalent to those in the human ankle and heel. A horse also has no muscles in its legs below the knees and hocks, only skin, hair, bone, tendons, ligaments, cartilage, and the assorted specialized tissues that make up the hoof.

The hoof is one of the most important to study, and easily damaged parts of a horse. The critical importance of the feet and legs is summed up by the traditional adage, 'no foot, no horse.' The exterior hoof wall and horn of the sole is made of essentially the same material as a human fingernail. The end result is that a horse, weighing on average 500 kilograms (1,100 lb), travels on the same bones as would a human on tiptoe. For the protection of the hoof under certain conditions, some horses have horseshoes placed on their feet by a professional farrier. The hoof continually grows, and in most domesticated horses needs to be trimmed (and horseshoes reset, if used) every five to eight weeks, though the hooves of horses in the wild wear down and regrow at a rate suitable for their terrain.

One of the most important aspects of equine care is farriery. Farriers have largely replaced blacksmiths (after this specialism largely became redundant after the industrial revolution), and are highly skilled in both metalwork and horse anatomy. Historically, the jobs of farrier and blacksmith were practically synonymous, shown by the etymology of the word: farrier comes from Middle French *ferrier* (blacksmith), and from the Latin word *ferrum* (iron). Modern day farriers usually specialize in horseshoeing though, focusing their time and effort on the care of the horse's hoof, including trimming and balancing of the hoof, as well as the placing of the shoes. Additional tasks for the farrier include dealing with injured or diseased hooves and application of special shoes for racing, training or 'cosmetic' purposes. In countries such as the United Kingdom, it is illegal for people other than registered farriers to call themselves a farrier or to carry out any farriery work, the primary aim being 'to prevent and avoid suffering by and cruelty to horses arising from the shoeing of horses by unskilled persons.' This is not the case in all countries however, where horse protection is severely lacking.

The terrain horses originally inhabited is crucial to understanding their anatomy; horses are naturally grazing creatures. In an adult horse, there are 12 incisors at the front of the mouth, adapted to biting off the grass or other vegetation, with 24 teeth adapted for chewing. Stallions and geldings have four additional teeth just behind the incisors, a type of canine teeth called 'tushes.' Some horses, both male and female, will also develop one to four very small vestigial teeth in front of the molars, known as 'wolf' teeth, which are generally removed because they can interfere with the bit. As horses are herbivores, their grazing nature has resulted in a digestive system adapted to steady consumption of grasses. Therefore, compared to humans, they have a relatively small stomach but very long intestines to facilitate a steady flow of nutrients. Interestingly, horses are unable to vomit – so digestion problems can arise quickly, causing colic, a leading killer.

Horse breeds are loosely divided into three categories based on general temperament: spirited 'hot bloods' with speed and endurance; 'cold bloods', such as draft horses and some ponies, suitable for slow, heavy work; and 'warm bloods', developed from crosses between hot bloods and cold bloods, often focusing on creating breeds for specific riding purposes, particularly in Europe. There are more than 300 breeds of horse in the world today, developed for many different uses. The concept of purebred bloodstock and a controlled, written breed registry has become particularly significant; sometimes inaccurately described as 'thoroughbreds'. Thoroughbred is a specific breed of horse, while a 'purebred' is a horse (or any other animal) with a defined pedigree recognized by a breed registry. An early example of people who practiced selective horse breeding were the Bedouin, who had a reputation for careful practices, keeping extensive pedigrees of their Arabian horses and placing great value upon pure bloodlines. In the fourteenth century, Carthusian monks of southern Spain kept meticulous pedigrees of bloodstock lineages still found today in the Andalusian horse.

We hope the reader enjoys this book, and is encouraged to explore the world of horse breeding and anatomy for themselves.

FOREWORD

No one has done more—in Australia, at any rate—to substantiate the claims of the Arab horse than the veteran statesman of South Australia, Sir James Boucaut, both by his writings and through the establishment of the Quambi stud, which he maintained for many years at Mount Barker Springs in South Australia. His former book on the subject, published in 1905, attracted widespread attention in Great Britain, America, and the Commonwealth, and his opinions were, I believe, endorsed by a very large majority of experts. From those who resented any reflection upon their theories or methods some criticism was to be expected. With that the present volume effectually deals.

That the selection of the so-called "thoroughbred" purely for speed has been detrimental to horseflesh in general admits of no doubt. Lack of stamina is the common defect. If the thoroughbred were intended solely for racing, this might be of little consequence, but surely the legitimate function of the thoroughbred is to serve as the stock for improving general utility horses. As Sir Walter Gilbey has observed, " two-year-old races, short distances and light-weights, leave all the best qualities of horseflesh untaxed. They do more: they tend to develop delicacy of constitution." Many who breed horses for the Turf do not even pretend to aim at effecting the improvement of horses apart from racing purposes. Isolated owners have broader views, and a few follow the admirable example of breeding in various classes for all-round excellence set by His Majesty the King. The vast majority, however, of breeders have no such idea; too many of them regard the horse as an instrument of racing, and perhaps of gambling, pure and simple. To such persons the Turf is merely the green cloth on a larger scale. Eliminate betting and the racecourse would, I fear, have a desperate struggle for existence. But of this being done there is not the least likelihood. The community, therefore, owes a deep debt of gratitude to men with the knowledge and experience of Sir James Boucaut, when they point out the attendant evils, and indicate, as forcibly as he does, the steps required to bring about a better state of things.

In its military bearings the need for reform is of supreme importance. The continued shortage in the supply of suitable army remounts is a grave danger, and it cannot be removed without the adoption of some definite policy of reform. Horses of varying characteristics are needed, and they cannot be obtained by haphazard breeding. The chief deficiency appears to exist in what may be termed " intermediate horses "—that is, in the cross between a sound thoroughbred and a carefully selected mare of heavier stamp. By careful selection and breeding we have been able to produce many varieties of cattle and sheep true to type, and it should be possible to do the same with horses. The experiments now being conducted in the application of the Mendelian principles to horse-breeding may solve the problem. I do not think it is at all safe to ignore the example of foreign countries. The Arab stallions at the national studs in France, Austria, Hungary, Italy, Russia, and Turkey have proved of incalculable benefit.

To the Australian continent the Arab is particularly

FOREWORD

adapted. On the great plains of the remote interior the distances to be traversed are enormous, and can only be covered by animals capable of travelling at a fair pace all day and for days together upon scanty rations. In a unique degree the Arab possesses these qualifications. Its powers of endurance, docility, and hardiness are proverbial. I think abundant evidence of this will be found in this book. No allusion, however, is made, I think, to the famous match in Egypt, in 1864, between an Arab horse and an English mare. The race was one of eighty-four miles from Suez to Cairo. The Arab, which was of the Anazeh breed, completed the journey in less than eight hours, whereas the mare collapsed at the sixtieth mile.

It is a pleasure to write these few lines in support of Sir James Boucaut's contentions, whose force is obvious to a reader who is not an expert. My sole desire is to recommend to notice a matter which I regard as of the deepest interest, not only to the Mother Country, but also to Australia and to the Empire at large. I cannot refrain from expressing my admiration of the spirit displayed by my old friend, who, after a strenuous and brilliant career in the arena of politics followed by twenty-seven years as a Judge of the Supreme Court, brings his first-class fighting qualities to bear on a matter of serious moment to our national and Imperial welfare.

Many will agree with the author in his belief that the best mode of improving our horses would be " the infusion of a large amount of pure and fresh Arab blood of the desert breed."

G. H. REID.

PREFACE

I MUST crave the indulgence of the public for a considerable lack of finish in this volume, probably some repetition, and possibly some mistakes in dates and in the spelling of names. These errors, however, are not in themselves serious, and do not affect the general accuracy of the book. My excuse is that I had to choose between publishing the manuscript as it is and abandoning it altogether. At the age of eighty, and subject to repeated attacks of illness, I am quite unable to undertake the task of careful revision which I had intended. The work of verifying and comparing references is beyond my strength. I have decided, therefore, to publish the book at once, since I am anxious that the admirers of that grand creature, the Arab, should be in possession of further information to weigh against "the enemy." At the same time, I wish my farming friends in the country to have full opportunity of learning what may be useful to them, but is not at present sufficiently brought to their notice. Information even badly arranged is better than no information.

I should add that the facts mentioned are for the most part entirely new, and not a mere repetition of my former book. I desire to express my grateful thanks to the High Commissioner for Australia, Sir George Reia, for writing a foreword to this little volume, and to Sir John Cockburn and Mr. J. C. Medd for kind assistance in seeing it through the press.

JAMES PENN BOUCAUT.

November, 1911.

CONTENTS

CHAPTER		PAGE
	FOREWORD	v
	PREFACE	ix
I.	INTRODUCTION	1
II.	SOME TESTIMONY TO THE ARAB'S EXCELLENCE	5
III.	A REVIEW OF SOME OF THE CRITICISMS OF MY FORMER BOOK	9
IV.	DISPERSAL OF MY PURE STUD	22
V.	THE ARAB A LOW HORSE	29
VI.	UNIFORM EXCELLENCE OF ARABS GATHERED FROM VARIOUS AUTHORS	44
VII.	EXCELLENCE OF THE ARAB, GATHERED CHIEFLY FROM VARIOUS NEWSPAPERS AND MAGAZINES	77
VIII.	ARAB HORSES AS PRESENTS	91
IX.	ARAB HORSES IN ENGLAND IN EARLY TIMES	97
X.	MR. WILFRID BLUNT AND PROFESSOR RIDGEWAY	100
XI.	HORSES IN ANCIENT ARABIA	108
XII.	AN OUTLINE SKETCH OF SOME EASTERN HISTORY	120
XIII.	A WORD OR TWO CONCERNING REVERSION	128
XIV.	THE THOROUGHBRED	134
XV.	DETERIORATION, AS GATHERED FROM THE "TIMES"	142
XVI.	DETERIORATION, AS GATHERED FROM THE "AUSTRALASIAN"	172
XVII.	DETERIORATION, AS GATHERED FROM NEWSPAPERS GENERALLY	191
XVIII.	DETERIORATION ACCORDING TO SUNDRY BOOKS AND MAGAZINES	197
XIX.	HORSE-RACING	204
XX.	CONCLUSION	218

THE ARAB HORSE

CHAPTER I

INTRODUCTION

SEVERAL books dealing more or less with the Arab horse have appeared in recent years, and since the publication of my book in 1905, Professor Ridgeway has compiled a most learned work on the " Origin and Influence of the Thoroughbred Horse." There are also " The Horses of the British Empire," edited by Sir Humphrey de Trafford, and " Eclipse and O'Kelly," by Theodore Andrea Cook, which also bear considerably on the subject.

But these are all written from a different standpoint from that from which I write; all, with the exception of Professor Ridgeway's work, are too expensive for most farmers to purchase, and, further, they are somewhat unwieldy. I write with the desire to show my farming friends that the Arab is the best general utility horse in the world,—the glory of horsedom,—and for the information of many farming friends who have been taught to prefer a big, leggy half-bred to a pure-bred little Arab, I may say, the opinions which I expressed in my former book have been greatly strengthened by reading, experience and inquiry. My profession has taught me to be sceptical, and one of its axioms is never to take anything for granted; but I acknowledge to being overwhelmed with astonishment at the wonderful history of the Arab horse, and at the consensus of opinion for over five thousand years—I believe, nearer ten—that he is not only unexcelled, but that he has not been ever equalled, or even approached, in the world's history.

The works which I have mentioned above, although they do not ignore the Arab horse—indeed, they often greatly praise him,—make him quite a secondary object. One or two of these writers seem to have imbibed something of the spirit of the late William Day, the great trainer, who said that, for the practical purpose of bettering the thoroughbred, the Arab was as dead as the Dodo. Of course he was wrong, although he only referred to bettering the thoroughbred for modern racing purposes, which is a belief naturally adopted by most racing men who are content with what they are told by trainers and jockeys who, as a rule, estimate a horse by his speed, and think no more of a pure-blood Arab than they do of the sorriest weed—indeed, for the matter of that, they would think more of a goat if they could win more money with it. The Arab, they say, is dead, so far as bettering the thoroughbred is concerned, not because the latter is incapable of improvement, but because the breeders will not use him for that purpose, as it would require two or three descents to make the Arab blood sufficiently tell to make his speed equal to that of the thoroughbred over five or six furlongs. The majority of racing-men aim at getting sprinters at two years old or so. There is little chance, therefore, of their using the Arab which has not been bred for sprinting, and is of slower growth, although there are instances of recent Arab crosses being successful on the racecourse.

I contend that the Arab horse is the best in the world for all purposes for which he is fitted, or for which the thoroughbred is fitted, except sprinting. I maintain that the thoroughbred horse, take him in the aggregate, is by comparison an ill-bred creature, practically useless

INTRODUCTION

for all other purposes than sprinting, save when, as in one case out of a hundred, you get an Ormonde or a Persimmon, and neither of these or their stock are perfect, nor can any of them always be relied on. This is because the thoroughbred is, in truth, a mongrel, and you can never rely on a mongrel to breed true. I further contend that it is impossible for any indifferent man to read what I have collected and here set forth about the thoroughbred without seeing that as a breed he is unreliable, and that, unless the present style of breeding be altered, he will become at his very best useless except for gambling, as many undoubted authorities whom I cite are found emphatically to declare. I rely on the weight of the authorities whom I quote—many of them of the highest class—and I make no claim to personal knowledge of racing. I submit many of our leading writers approach the subject with by far too much prejudice and too little genuine inquiry to do the Arab justice. I have been astonished at the ignorance shown by men who ought to know better. One gentleman, for instance, in a letter to a great daily Australian paper to correct my book, stated that an Arab could not be safely ridden in hilly country because for thousands of years he had been used only to travel in a smooth, soft, sandy desert ! which is a grotesque misstatement. Yet many are of this opinion. Arab horses regularly travel amongst hills, rocks and precipices where no English rider would venture to ride a thoroughbred, for one could never depend on his evenness of temper. In many parts of Arabia and on its borders there are most dangerous hills and precipices, and the descriptions of them by many travellers will be found herein. Since the above letter, I came across a book on Armenia, by the Hon. Robert Curzon, which tells us that on a road, just wide enough for one horse, passing through streams, over rocks, mountains and precipices, where you would imagine that a goat could hardly travel, and where you wonder how in the world you ever got to the place you are standing on, the surefootedness of the horses was marvellous. He saw a horse at a particularly dangerous spot rest on his haunches and put forward one foot to feel if it were safe. Another road he describes as like walking on the rounds of a ladder.

One especially wise man of the East wrote to a newspaper in New South Wales protesting against my book, because his conscience would not let him remain silent when he saw that I was advising low horses for the army! I rather admire that gentleman's conscience, but it must be a sad trouble to him sometimes. He said it was "dreadful" to think of our brave soldiers going into action on low horses. Some people get funny ideas into their heads. Nearly every soldier of mark in the empire denounces high horses as being totally unfit for campaigning, as this book will show.

CHAPTER II

SOME TESTIMONY TO THE ARAB'S EXCELLENCE

I WROTE my former book because I had formed the opinion that undue praise was being accorded to the thoroughbred at the expense of the Arab horse, although the former has greatly deteriorated, and that the great excellence of the Arab was practically ignored—facts which, being an Englishman, were burnt into me, so to speak, by the Transvaal War, the iron whereof entered into my soul, and I desired again to call the attention of all those who wanted general utility horses in Australia to the Arab.

That my book was not calculated to do any harm may be gathered from the fact that Sir Walter Gilbey wrote me a preface, for which I record my very grateful thanks, and that it was calculated to do some good is clear from the review of the *Times*, which I set forth here as an appendix, separate and apart from the general mass of newspaper reviews and criticisms which I shall cite later on. I was more gratified by that review in the *Times* than by any other laudatory remarks (although they were many), for the *Times* is admittedly the greatest newspaper in the world. It is invariably careful, desirous of being as far as possible accurate, and its policy is always to be judicial, fair and level-headed, while the ablest and the best-informed writers are proud to write for it.

Thus, then, says the *Times*, September 22, 1905 :—

"Sir James Boucaut, an expert and an enthusiast, has written a most instructive volume on ' The Arab ' (Gay and Bird), and in almost all he says we can heartily agree, except in his confidence that the Arab is the horse of the future. We wish it may be so, but, so far as the British Isles are concerned, we fear the future is in the far distance. So much he indirectly admits himself, in dwelling on the magnitudes of the evils he would fain remedy, and the dry-rot which has been steadily diffusing itself through English and Australian stables. Sir James, who, like Mr. Scawen Blunt in Egypt and Sussex, has amused himself by breeding Arabs in Southern Australia, is not the first by many who has preached deterioration in our thoroughbred or prescribed reverting to Arab blood as a remedy. No one has studied the subject more deeply or spoken more emphatically than Sir Walter Gilbey, who contributes the preface and endorses the contents of Sir James's book. As for the deterioration at home, it has been practically admitted by the most capable authorities, and we have had painful experience of it in the increasing difficulty of mounting our cavalry ; but we were not aware that Australia had been following suit, though we might have surmised as much, for the best Australian stock has been bred from imported mares and sires. But Sir James Boucaut mentions a startling fact. Forty years ago or less, next to the pure Arab, the Waler was the favourite mount for pigsticking. Now we are told that the Waler is condemned in the pigsticking clubs as washy, weedy and worthless. If there is little doubt as to the decline of the thoroughbred, there is less as to the cause. The racing market is infinitely the most remunerative, and there the imperative demand is for length, legs and precocious pace. The demand is for the multiplication of the money-making type of breed, and that is why we misdoubt the approximate advent of the Arab. The Arab is low as lasting, his quality is

TESTIMONY TO THE ARAB'S EXCELLENCE 7

endurance rather than pace ; and, ever since Charles II. patronized Newmarket and racing, we have been grading up our thoroughbreds. Nor would the pure Arab be a profitable stock-getter for horses meant for the hunting-field or the park. Fourteen or fifteen hands is hardly the stamp of horse to fly the wide pastures of the Midlands. Nevertheless, we thoroughly agree with Sir James in everything he says in praise of his favourites. For spirit, endurance, intelligence, docility, and the capacity for severe and prolonged work on scanty commons, they are unsurpassed, and, as to that, from an almost unexampled range of reading he calls up a cloud of unimpeachable witnesses.

" If we again took to importing Arab blood, we should only be imitating the good sense of our ancestors. We all know that the Byerly Turk and Darley and Godolphin Arabians were the progenitors of our most famous racers ; but few are aware that King John of ambiguous memory conferred an inestimable boon on his country as a generous importer of Eastern sires, and that the importation he encouraged went steadily on till the trade was paralyzed by the Wars of the Roses. With regard to the all-important question of mounting our cavalry, there is one episode to which Sir James reverts repeatedly as a crucial example of the superexcellence of the Arab. He quotes from Mr. Stevens' 'With Kitchener to Khartoum.' Stevens tells us how our heavy Dragoons who, with their innumerable encumbrances, rode from 18 to 20 stone, had left their chargers in Cairo, as unsuited to the country and unequal to the weight. On the advance to Omdurman they were mounted on little Syrian ponies —part Arab—which did the work gamely without giving in. We might add some evidence of our own as to the virtues of the ubiquitous Arab strain. We know something of the little horses of the Pyrenees and of the ponies of the Ardennes. Both trace their descent through Spain to Africa and Arabia. The ponies of the Ardennes are well cared for ; the horses of the Pyrenees are stabled on furze and often half-famished. Yet it is well-nigh impossible in the longest and hardest day to get to the bottom of either, and, however jaded the little beast may seem, the fire flashes up on the slightest excitement."

Such a notice would give any author satisfaction, and it deserves the careful attention of all who seek to know the truth.

CHAPTER III

A REVIEW OF SOME OF THE CRITICISMS OF MY FORMER BOOK

Of course, my book was attacked by some of the sporting newspapers, although most of those which I saw were fair, and some, indeed, were much more commendatory than I had expected. I cannot trouble my readers with comments on the criticisms, but one sapient " sport " in Australia particularly amused me, and compels me to call attention to the speciality of my book, which is its reference to practical authorities and innumerable expert and experienced men. The " sport " referred to wrote that my book was not much good, because it was entirely built of statements made by other persons. I wonder what the gentleman could have expected, or what he would desire? I could not give what history has affirmed about the Arab horse without quoting the statements of other people, nor could anyone else. I was not at the Battle of Damascus, when the Arabs destroyed the Roman power in Asia Minor, and every rider of a pure Arab horse was awarded double spoil ; nor was I with Napoleon Buonaparte in Syria or Egypt, when he stated that the Mamelukes on their Syrian Arabs were better mounted than the French cavalry, although the Syrian Arabs are not of pure blood ; nor was I recently with Abdur Rahman, Ameer of Afghanistan, when, on " his little Arab," he rode his escort to an absolute standstill, his men and their horses being alike unable to keep on their feet or to rise. " My own little Arab," says he, " alone remained standing."

Most people have to rely entirely on the statements of others for particulars of this nature, and, so far as I can judge, the statements made by others form the best part of the book, and are presented to my readers as being so, for I never made any claim to originality.

The account given of some particular and notable incident by a traveller who was not thinking of an Arab horse, or, indeed, of any horse at all, and who was not writing a book about horses, but whose attention was unexpectedly drawn to some great excellence of the Arab beyond that of horses in general, is of more than ordinary value, because it is spontaneously forced upon the writer, as it were, and is genuine. An incident thus casually mentioned is much more reliable than the praises of his " most excellent beast " by a horse-dealer anxious to sell his broken-down thoroughbred, or by a breeder with a fad.

For this reason, I set forth the opinions given me by various purchasers of my pure-blood Arab stallions between 1898 and 1908, most of them volunteered, and sent to me without being asked for. Men who are anxious to sell a horse naturally " crack him up," and one cannot always be quite certain that they do not exaggerate. Probably some do; but men who have bought a horse and then speak well of him, and are anxious to keep him, and become desirous of getting another similar one, are to be relied upon. Their interest in negotiating another purchase would be not to pass encomiums upon their earlier purchase, but rather to depreciate it, so as to get the new horse for less money. Their good opinions are therefore the more reliable.

CRITICISMS OF MY FORMER BOOK

Most of the purchasers of my pure-blood stallions are large breeders of horses in what is termed " The Bush," occupying many scores of square miles in the interior of Australia—men who are not so severely bitten with the racing mania as to be so jealous of the Arab as so many others seem to be.

Thus do these purchasers report :—

S. P. Mackay, Esq., of Brunswick, Melville Park, N.W. Australia, who purchased two—Saladin and Jedaan—in 1898 :—

" They are sleek as hounds ; never had a toothful except the natural herbage. I hear great accounts of Saladin's stock. Jedaan has grown a fine animal ; his stock are very promising and handsome as paint, and I am sorry I have not more of them."

This gentleman writes again, August 22, 1902 :—

" I hear great accounts of Saladin's stock. Jedaan is here under my eye, and is everything I could wish ; his stock are good and showy as well. . . . I am sure his stock will come out on top. I never made a purchase that has given me more satisfaction."

And again, September 15, 1903, Mr. Mackay writes :—

" Jedaan is very much to the fore at present this winter. I have broken in five only of his progeny to the buggy—four-year-olds—: two of them after driving them only four weeks I sold for £50. The others I am constantly driving, and they do their work splendidly, notwithstanding that most of the Bush roads are only sand. They are absolutely stanch, and have no vice ; they carry themselves so well that it pays to put nice harness on them."

And being in Adelaide on March 22, 1905, Mr. Mackay called on the breeder to say how much pleased he was with the young stock ; they were admired by everyone.

Mr. Mackay casually met Mr. Whitham, Inspector of

Education, about February 27, 1907, at Aldgate, and told him that some of Rafyk's stock had turned out splendidly ; that last season he had sold a young pair to the agent of a steam-shearing company to travel to a distant station shed, and they accomplished the journey of 500 miles in eight days, and showed no signs of being run down. He also said that his stallion Sheddon had taken first prize at the last Royal Agricultural Show at Perth.

F. S. Thompson, Esq., Warrawagine, Condon, N.W. Australia, who purchased Kazim :—

" Kazim continues to give us satisfaction ; as quiet as ever, and absolutely no vice. His young stock are doing well, and are satisfactory, those out of thoroughbred mares being especially good."

E. P. Quinn, Esq., of Tarella, Wilcannia, New South Wales, who purchased Assad :—

" Assad is growing into a fine horse, a nice shape, with really good legs, and bone like steel. His temper is all that could be desired. A more docile animal was never foaled, and yet he is full of fire and spirit."

Mr. Quinn has since purchased Adban. A friend casually heard in Melbourne that the manager of Salisbury Downs had ridden Assad throughout the drought, frequently getting over fifty and sixty miles in a day, and often at the end of a long journey he got very little feed, but next morning would start away quite fresh, and that he was positive he could not have done the work with the ordinary station-bred horse.

In subsequently inquiring what others were for sale, Mr. Quinn wrote, January 1, 1904 :—

" I am very pleased with the few Assads that I have ; they are nearly three years old now, and are all that could be desired ; they are handsome and very sturdy. Assad has stamped his stock very much after himself. Adban's stock are faultless as foals. I have nineteen head of as handsome foals by him as I would ever wish to see."

He has since bought a third youngster.

CRITICISMS OF MY FORMER BOOK

On March 11, 1904, he says :—

" I have all Assad's foals broken in ; they are all good hacks, very free and game, standing about 15 hands high. Adban's stock are beautiful, no doubt, and admired by everyone ; all fair size, very handsome and sturdy, good tempered as yearlings."

And on July 26, 1904, he writes :—

" Adban's stock are beauties, are handsome and good sorts. . . . I believe in the Arab blood for station horses, and think it is only a matter of a few years, and anyone, seeing the way they answer, will be sure and go in for them."

And on December 1, 1905, he writes :—

" I must continue to praise Adban, as no doubt he got very good stock. They are horses with any amount of size and substance, with quality combined. I cannot say enough about them, as regards their good qualities."

And on October 18, 1909, writing to tell me of the death of Ben Sira, he says :—

" Ben Sira was out in the paddock and jumped out : he then raced round and then made a big jump back again, and landed on a stump 5 feet high, which pierced through his hind part and tore him fearfully from the front of the sheath right to the butt of his tail. Death was almost instantaneous, thank Heaven. The last six months he had been developing into a beautiful animal, as handsome as a picture, so kind and docile we had grown to look on him as one of ourselves almost. The intelligence of poor Ben was almost human, and people say it is foolish to think of the loss of an animal, but I have been so attached to Ben the place is really lonely without him."

J. W. Brougham, Esq., of Poollamacca Station, Broken Hill, New South Wales, who purchased Abdallah, wrote :—

" Abdallah's stock promise well ; they are beautifully topped, with a fine carriage. His disposition is wonderfully quiet, and a child could ride him with safety."

On a later date he writes :—

"He is such a pet, ever so docile."

And on February 25, 1904, writing to thank me for a newspaper I sent him, adds :—

"It was rather strange, the day the newspaper arrived my boy brought in from the back station two of Abdallah's colts, just broken in. He was so proud of them he rode them in to show me, and really they show quality, breeding and usefulness. Perfect hacks, plenty of substance, standing 15½ hands, and only three years (off). Am breaking them in now, and when quiet will let them run till five years, then they will be fit for any work. I would like you to see the youngsters, and you would still be prouder of Rafyk."

N.B.—This supports Mr. Vincent Dowling, who stated that it was a great mistake to say that the foals got by Arab horses were too small.

On October 30, 1905, he met my son and told him that he was very much pleased with Abdallah's stock—that he was just the horse for that country.

And he informs me that Mr. D. Evans rode two Arab horses bred at Poolamacca in May, 1907, on the first day twenty-two miles, next day forty-five miles, and back, making ninety miles before the horses got water. Next day to Mr. Bull, where they would not drink the well-water, next day Wykalpa and back again to Border Tank, ninety-four miles. The horses had no water for 109 miles, two days and two nights, and yet showed no signs of distress.

Mr. C. R. Bunbury, of Williambury, West Australia, who purchased Khaled, wrote :—

"I like Khaled very well indeed. He is full of life and quality and his foals are very handsome. He is very docile when handled and a good goer."

And since then he writes, on September 12, 1903 :—

"I have broken in a dozen of Khaled's stock lately; they are the quietest and most tractable youngsters I

CRITICISMS OF MY FORMER BOOK

ever had anything to do with, and stand their work well for youngsters."

And again, July 7, 1908 :—

"I enclose a photo of my team of six half-bred Arabs by Khaled. I think it would be rather difficult to find a team of horses to beat this. I can drive them off the road as well as on it, and can drive anywhere where it is possible for a vehicle to go. They also do big journeys. I did eighty-four miles with them in nine hours' travelling; and, coming from Carnarvon with a very heavily loaded buggy, came home the last day, a journey of fifty miles, despite the fact they got nothing to eat except a bit of scrub. I should like to get another Arab stallion if you have one for sale."

Mr. Warburton, a horsebreeder in Northern Australia (who desired to purchase Zubeir), writes :—

"I very much regret my agents could not induce you to sell Zubeir, except under conditions that put me clean out of the running. It has been a great disappointment to me, as I had set my heart on getting him. Will you allow me to congratulate you on being the owner of such a horse as Rafyk? I can only say that words fail me to express my admiration for him. I could have spent hours looking at him. There is not such another horse in Australia ; he is perfect in every way."

[The conditions were that he was to remain at Quambi till two mares, Labahda and Sherifa, were stinted, but the writer has since purchased him.]

He further writes, May, 1904 :—

"Zubeir is growing very like Rafyk, and is in good trim. He has not had an ounce of stable feed since he has been up here. He is doing good work, and it would take a big cheque to buy him now."

He further writes :—

"As far as Zubeir and his stock go, the Arab deserves all the praise you give him in your book. Some of his youngsters, getting on for three years old, are perfect pictures."

And on April 11, 1906, when writing in respect of the purchase of another stallion, Mr. Warburton's agents, Messrs. Barker Bros., say :—

"Mr. Warburton writes in very eulogistic terms of Zubeir's progeny."

And on June, 1906 :—

"Mr. Warburton purchased another stallion—Darub."

And in a letter to Messrs. Barker Bros. of this city, dated July 9, 1809, Mr. Warburton states :—

"Darub is growing into a beautiful colt—all fire and quality."

Robert Bush, Esq., of Clifton Downs Station, Western Australia, says of Suleiman :—

"Having used him for about one year, I am unable of course to say anything about his stock. . . . I think he will mate well with the class of mares I have put to him. He is a beautiful-tempered horse and a good doer, having to cut his own grass ever since I have had him."

And again on July 6, 1903 :—

"Sulieman is doing very well, and I like his stock very much. Although he is small, his stock are of good size, and if they turn out as well as they look they will be very good. . . . There is no doubt at all that they will turn out well. Sulieman is a beautiful-tempered horse."

Mr. Creed, of Cecilwood, Rockhampton, purchaser of Barak, then just arrived in Rockhampton, writes, July 4, 1903 :—

"I think him a very handsome colt, and should make a very perfect horse. Everyone that has seen him thinks him a fine colt. . . . I am sure there will be no such horse in looks, style, etc., about here. I am very pleased with him."

CRITICISMS OF MY FORMER BOOK

He also writes, December 13, 1907 :—
"I told you when I first saw Barak that I thought he would make a perfect horse, and I am quite satisfied now that he has done so. He is about as muscular a horse as could be, of beautiful colour, and carries himself in great style, and what is more, he is throwing it into his stock. He is about as sure foal-getter as possible, and from those who have got foals by him I have never heard one disparaging remark. He is a general favourite with everyone."

Mr. T. H. Pearce, of the Katherine, says of Ibrahim and Joktan :—
"They give every satisfaction. I am delighted with them."

He bought them without seeing them, from his faith in the blood, as indeed did most of these purchasers.

Mr. Edwin Crozier, who bought Morad, writes, April 29, 1906 :—
"I am very pleased to tell you that Morad has done well since I got him, and has thickened out very considerably. I am much pleased with his looks. I may say that I have had him ridden. He is very playful, but, so far as I can see, absolutely free from vice, has not the slightest sense of fear, and his carriage is perfect."

And since that purchase I am informed that Mr. Crozier bought Amezeh, which I sold to a lady who subsequently died.

R. Maitland, Esq., Maryborough, Queensland, writes of Hunyar and Naish, September 13, 1906 :—
"You will be pleased to know that both colts have done well since they came over here, and are much admired as very fine specimens of their breed."

Mr. Isaac Henderson, Ardrossan, who bought Mesrour, writes, July 15, 1907 :—
"My little Arab colt, Mesrour, is doing splendidly. All who see him admire his graceful manners. I love him immensely."

And on January 26, 1910, Mr. Henderson called upon me at my chambers to let me know that Mesrour is quiet and much admired, and getting popular as a sire by reason of the excellence of his stock. Mr. Henderson often rides him. He has a notable love of turning; he turns in his own length at full gallop.

Half-breeds I have not kept account of, but the late G. H. Ayliffe, Esq. (Registrar-General of Births), says:—

"Young Jericho (half-Arab, half-thoroughbred) has greatly surpassed our expectations in quality, temper and endurance. We experienced not the slightest trouble in breaking him to and driving him in single and double harness, and he is very quiet in the stable. As a proof of his powers of endurance, I may mention that on a very hot day last summer he carried me (over thirteen stone weight) nearly sixty miles through the hills with only one short stoppage to feed, and arrived home so fresh that I feel confident he could have gone twenty or thirty miles further without greatly distressing himself. I have some foals by him, which are showing excellent form as regards size and points."

Lieutenant Fotheringham says of one of Rafyk's get:—

"The best pony he has ever owned or sat behind, her temper was perfect and endurance unsurpassed. Rafyk was the sire."

Mr. Edwin Wilcox writes of another of Rafyk's get:—

"A magnificent fellow ... very handsome ... in harness and saddle very docile."

Mr. A. J. McDonald, the Manager of the Great Canowie Station, on January 9, 1908, writes me with respect to Nejan, an imported Arab stallion, purchased from Mr. Blunt:—

"I am well satisfied not only with the horse himself but with his progeny also. His prepotency is most pronounced; no matter what class of mare he is mated with, the issue is good and characteristic of himself; and in most cases courage, carriage and animal spirit are striking

CRITICISMS OF MY FORMER BOOK

features of his get. Though high spirited, they are of docile temperament, and in conformation, bone and substance fill the bill ; especially is this so when mated with our Suffolk cross-bred mares. There are Arabs and so-called Arabs, but the pure-bred Desert Arab has no superior for pluck and endurance and the faculty of transmitting these qualities to his offspring."

I was favoured with a copy of a report, February 5, 1904, by Mr. A. H. Morris, who was sent to inspect my stud, in which he writes :—

"Rafyk is a powerful horse, and I like him very much. Faraoun is a shade finer in bone than Rafyk, shows more quality about the head ; he is a beautifully-made horse and worth a day's journey to look at. If you get a chance, go out and see him. He is a beauty. The pure-bred Arab mares are a nice lot, but Rose of Jericho is quality all over. There are two nice yearling colts (pure Arabs), but both are sold. I saw three geldings, out of Stud Book mares, one that I wish had been kept for a stallion. He would have suited me. He is out of a thoroughbred mare, but has the stout body of an Arab ; he is a powerful horse—I like him very much. I have seen that the cross between the thoroughbred mare and Arab is a splendid cross. The other gelding—a chestnut—is lengthy, lean and wiry ; but if he is not a hard, wiry horse and a fast one, I am much mistaken. I thoroughly enjoyed myself to-day. I wish I had money for what I could do in the shape of producing horses that would not only be useful, but would give pleasure to look at."

(Neither the writer of the report nor his principal was known to the owner of the stud.)

Mr. G. Leonard Brown, of Wirronna, New South Wales, who bought Faraoun at my dispersal sale, writes me :—

"Faraoun is as quiet as a lamb. I ride him bare-backed at the canter and jump on and off as he careers along, much to his delight, as he squeaks in joy from time to time."

And he proposes sending to Mr. Wilfred Blunt in Sussex for some more mares.

In September, 1909, Dr. Jude, formerly of Adelaide, now of White Cliffs, New South Wales, introduced Mr. Byers of that place to me, who told me that he had bought one of my pure-bred stallions, Assad, from Mr. Quinn, of Tarella, to whom I sold him, and that he was very much pleased with him. He said that about the end of July, 1908, in a matter of life and death, he sent Assad with a stock-keeper from White Cliffs to Morden, fifty miles away, for medicine. The rider weighed thirteen stone. He started in the morning and was back the same evening, doing the double journey in about thirteen hours, and Assad had no food on the road. Mr. Byers mentioned that Assad's stock are exceedingly good and of remarkable docility.

Mr. Maughan, a professional gentleman of Adelaide whom I did not previously know, on April 11, 1909, saw Rafferty, belonging to Mr. Hickes, of Mount Torrens, by Rafyk out of a roadster mare, and called to tell me that Rafferty is very docile and throws splendid stock; he comes galloping up to you in the paddock when called. He is a most perfect hack—"like a rocking horse"—a bright chestnut about 15·2; he was never in harness, but has splendid action.

Mr. A. R. Crawford, a well-known breeder of New South Wales, on a visit to Mr. J. Fitzgerald's station at East Kunderang, writes me that Kahtan by Rafyk, foaled August 25, 1907, is doing finely, is very gentle, a great pet, and in fine condition, though not at all pampered, and will make a powerful weight-carrying horse, fit to produce Army remounts. Mr. Crawford adds that the English thoroughbred is still jogging on in the old way—heart disease, breaking bloodvessels, shoulders and legs, and getting worse. He denounces stallions by St. Simon as the most ill-tempered lot the world has seen in our time.

Mr. Joseph Fitzgerald, of Kunderang East Station, New South Wales, on January 12, 1911, writes that Kahtan has grown into a beautiful horse, with as much strength in body and legs, and character as the best judge could desire; he has a beautiful disposition, a stylish carriage and plenty of life; still, he can be ridden barebacked. "I have a few foals by him all showing energy, activity, intelligence, style and strength."

CHAPTER IV

DISPERSAL OF MY PURE STUD

I WAS exceedingly sorry to feel it desirable to disperse my pure Arab stud, but with the weight of seventy-eight years upon me and with failing health, and my stud farm being in the hills over thirty miles from my residence, I found it not only a difficulty to get there, but a greater difficulty to ride about in the paddocks as freely as I would wish, and as I had been used to do. Indeed, it was my main pleasure in life to ride to my paddocks and walk amongst my mares and have them come up to me and rub my shoulder. But my managing son, being an admirer of sheep and not of horses, confided to me that he would not be a horse-breeder, so I had no alternative but to disperse my stud, keeping, however, a couple of mares for a grandson and one as company for myself.

I hope to be excused for having inserted the statements in the last chapter, they being a collection of other men's opinions. But when twenty or thirty or more gentlemen, having intimate practical knowledge of the subject, affirm that the Arab is a most excellent horse and throws splendid stock, then it is desirable that all honest breeders should give some consideration to what those gentlemen say, and indeed not merely consider it, but carefully study it. Even supposing there be one " frigid liar " and two

DISPERSAL OF MY PURE STUD

silly dreamers amongst them—which I deny—they cannot all be liars or dreamers.

There are assuredly some level-headed men who will take facts into their consideration, even if they own racehorses, and although I shall have a certain measure of joy should there be only one "ignorant person who repenteth," yet I shall live in hopes—if I live at all after writing this book—that a good many will be advantaged by the further information which I shall place at their service. "One swallow does not make a summer," so one poem—even Job's—on a horse may not be conclusive; but universal praise during at the very least two thousand years, probably during the last five thousand, and possibly during the last ten thousand, by all who knew—many of them the best horsemen the world ever saw, men who lived on horseback, nations of horsemen from the Far East in China to the Far West at the Pillars of Hercules—will be entirely rejected only by fools, or by the other sort of creature.

The most extraordinary thing that I have noticed in the discussion about the Arab is the bitterness of spirit which is shown by many of those who oppose his claims to excellence. They show no bitterness of spirit when they say that the Suffolk Punch or the Shire horse cannot gallop as fast as the thoroughbred.

Why, then, show such bitterness in speaking of the Arab? He has done them no harm. That it is so is patent to all. Indeed, he has done them much good. He made their thoroughbred. Even upon a sober commission of wise and well-informed men this bitterness is found to creep out. For instance, one of the Peers who was on, or was a witness before, Lord Rosebery's Committee, complained of the deep-seated prejudice he had to meet whenever he alluded to the Arab.

Mr. Huntingdon, the great American breeder, also wrote to me complaining of this bitterness. On seeing my original book, he obtained from England five copies for his friends, and after reading it he sent to England for fifteen more copies for other friends. Farmers and general utility horse-breeders will see from this that there must be something about the Arab worth reading and studying to have induced a man of Mr. Huntington's reputation and judgment to act like this.

The reason for the complaint made by Mr. Huntingdon is plain, viz., that a positive jealousy of the Arab is felt in many quarters by men some of whom have great influence in forming public opinion, which almost always sets up certain authorities to be worshipped as unmeaningly as the Australian aboriginals worship their god Mumbo Jumbo, or obey the orders of their medicine man. There are two reasons which, unconsciously it may be, influence some gentlemen : first, their interests as breeders or racers of thoroughbreds, and, secondly, their long belief in their favourite strain, which pride or stubbornness will not allow to be shaken.

I wish—I say it with all grave and becoming respect, disclaiming emphatically any irreverence—that it were possible, for the good of the nation, that we could get the opinion of some entirely neutral person (say, for example, some great ecclesiastic, ignorant of horse-racing and not much acquainted with horses), on the dispute between the advocates of the thoroughbred and those of the Arab, to be given after careful consideration and according to the lessons of history and the experience of men who know. There would soon be a very different opinion abroad. If the proposed ecclesiastic agreed to ride in order to have a more satisfactory test, I think he would prefer to trust himself outside an Arab rather than on a thoroughbred.

DISPERSAL OF MY PURE STUD

But that is not possible. I now set forth various opinions of many of the newspapers of the day as to my former book. Press opinions of a book, even when favourable, do not always bear conclusively upon the discussion entered upon in that particular book. The Press, for example, might praise a book on biology as of unexampled cleverness or as deeply interesting, and yet state that the author was wrong from beginning to end. But here the Press statements happen to show directly that the author is right, not by their praise of his book, but of the Arab horse, the particular subject-matter which the book praises, and therefore I feel justified in citing them as authorities in the Arab's favour. I trust that farmers and country gentlemen who breed horses will recognize the force of these opinions. They cannot all be wrong. A farmer's son may scoff at Job and say, " O his is only one !"; but when almost thousands are brought before him, who say the very same, he will do sad injustice to our modern education system if he does not pay some consideration to the matter.

PRESS OPINIONS OF MY PREVIOUS BOOK

Pall Mall Gazette.—" The author has done a good service."

South Australian Register.—" An earnest, interesting work."

Leeds Mercury.—" The author abundantly proves that deterioration of thoroughbred horses exists to an alarming extent."

The Scotsman.—" The book merits earnest attention."

Glasgow Herald.—" It is to be hoped that the book will be carefully read."

The Sporting Times.—" No horse in the world is as good for pig-sticking purposes."

The Australasian.—" The book cannot fail to be both instructive and interesting."

The Yorkshire Post.—" Its lessons are worthy of note. There is abundant evidence of the value of a good Arab strain."

Bulletin.—" The old judge has not lost his trick of vigorous language."

Morning Post.—" This book will enable horse-breeders to understand the value of the Arab."

Dundee Advertiser.—" The book is well worth study, for the time has come to revert to the pure Arab."

Field.—" A case of great strength, both against the thoroughbred and in favour of the Arab."

South Australian Advertiser (London Correspondent).—" The book contains a great deal of sound sense."

Baily's Magazine.—" The Arab remains unspoiled, and if Sir James can induce colonial breeders to recognize his sterling merits he will have done a service not only to Australia, but even the Empire."

Irish Times.—" A valuable work."

Country Life.—" The Arab's docility, constitution, easy paces and hardiness commend him for many purposes."

The Standard.—" Sir James Boucaut forces upon our attention a state of affairs which is of national and Imperial importance."

New York Herald.—" In Arabia the horses maintain the qualities which are most useful in war horses, and, indeed, in all horses where gambling is not the main consideration."

Daily Telegraph (New South Wales).—" There is much put forward in the book which will take a great deal of answering."

The Referee, a sporting paper, admits that Arabs, more or less pure-bred, can go great distances, can endure great hardships, carry surprising weights for their size and build, are docile, plucky, and in character better adapted for campaigning over difficult country than the ordinary English cavalry remount. Their endurance is wonderful, and so is their power of living and feeding rough.

The Sportsman.—" There is, however, a certain amount of truth in the existence of the evil which he deplores."

The Asian.—" Breeding to the best type of the Arab will be the best means of checking degeneration, for in Arab horses we can get constitution, stamina, staying power, good bone, of the very highest quality and courage."

The Spectator.—" And long before the Christian era such horses were sought by horse lovers all over the Mediterranean and Western Asia. . . . With Sir James's main thesis we are in the fullest agreement."

Sporting Life.—" One would think that with such a variety of horse literature there was not a vacancy for Sir James Boucaut's work. As soon as we dip into the well-considered volume we are convinced that there was a vacancy, and that this book fills it."

The Sydney Morning Herald.—" The book is highly interesting and will prove valuable as a means of promoting discussion on the reintroduction of the Arab."

Daily Mail (Brisbane).—" Is refreshing reading. His work is valuable to breeders."

The Pastoralists' Review.—" In my opinion Sir James Boucaut's Arabs are going to shine in Australia, for my experience is that a man is never called on to take up his saddle and walk if his horse has a teaspoonful of Arab blood in his veins."

The Live Stock Journal (England).—" Australian breeders could not render greater service to themselves and to the Empire than to build upon a foundation of Arab blood. All men who cultivate close acquaintance with the Arab find that there is no breed to equal it in real work. We trust that his (Sir James Boucaut's) teaching may come home to a larger audience than that in his adopted home."

The Western Australian.—" Sir James Boucaut deserves well of his country in the first place for establishing a stud of pure Arabs accessible to all Australian breeders, and secondly for writing the book under review, which is a warning to our rulers to wake out of the indifference hitherto exhibited."

Daily Mail.—" From personal observation and experience, I have long urged an Arab development of horse stock for every purpose."

The Outlook.—" Of all horses he is the most companionable, not only because he is intelligent and stout-hearted, but on account of his indomitable cheeriness. You travel *on* other horses but *with* your Arab. Of the stoutness and soundness of the breed, of the ivory quality of the Arab bone, there has never been any question, and these characteristics they impart to their progeny."

I may add that in February, 1910, I received a letter from a gentleman in England previously unknown to me, who wrote me that my former book had twice been read through by him, a much occupied lover of horses, and that he had frequently heard it quoted. Indeed, he says: " My love for the Arab and its derivatives makes the book precious to me." The best small, compact horse known to him is the Connemara Hobby, which he largely praises, and of which he has a stud of the best procurable. He concludes by saying that if I would care to have one mare or stallion he would gladly give me a foal or filly. What praise can be more emphatic than that?

CHAPTER V

THE ARAB A LOW HORSE

THE Arab is a low horse. He is what the old bushmen of Australia of the forties and fifties, riders of half-bred Arabs, used to term a big horse in a little compass. They always preferred low horses. They knew the craze for tall horses is a huge mistake. You cannot possibly breed for speed and height without losing other more valuable qualities, as many breeders of thoroughbreds now admit, and this chapter will contain much matter which goes towards proving it. The constant reference to "little" horses and "small" horses shows that the writers using those words had been accustomed to big horses—their eyes had been accustomed to size—which made the feats of the smaller horses appear the more remarkable to them.

Their tastes had become depraved by love of bigness for bigness' sake. By-and-bye, in a generation or so, people will wonder how they came to be so unwise. If you had offered a stock-rider of the Bush in the forties a stock-horse of 16 hands and upwards for stock-riding, he would have considered himself insulted : he would have thought you were laughing at him.

In his book, "With the Khirgiz," Lord V. Beauclerk says that Khirgiz ponies, wiry, well-balanced little animals from $12\frac{1}{2}$ to $13\frac{1}{2}$ hands high, will climb all day, and their feet will last several weeks' work amongst the rocks. The regulation distance for a race in their country is thirteen to fourteen miles. The time, thirty-three minutes for the fourteen miles, seems extraordinarily good for a grass-fed pony of under 13 hands, and these weekly races have been held for generations by the natives at Kashgara. These ponies for many generations have been improved by Arab stallions.

In the *Argus* of February 19, 1906, Mr. William Day is cited as saying that you may get fifty small good horses for one good large one, and the former will do well after the latter has been put to the stud (*i.e.*, after he is done for as a racer). A good big horse, he says, may beat a good little one over a short course or even at a mile or so, but at three or four miles a good little one would beat the best big one he ever saw. In truth, the small horse seems to revert more to the Arab, the big horse to the Flanders mare.

The *Times* of January 1, 1906, says that :—

" A more suitable beast for mounted infantry than the Chinese pony is hardly conceivable—docile, easily trained, and easy to mount. The breed was improved by Arabs two milleniums ago."

On November 26, 1906, it wrote :—

" In the breeding of all classes of stock where prominent consideration is given to purity of blood and fineness of quality, there is a distinct tendency towards diminution in the size of the progeny, which suggests that size and quality are in a certain degree incompatible terms. The history of the polo pony itself furnishes proof of the contention that the maintenance of size is as difficult of attainment as uniformity in type."

Blackwood's Magazine for November, 1904, states that General McQueen, one of the ablest soldiers who ever commanded in the Punjab, rode not a superb charger which would be useless on the rough ground, but a small pony that could scramble over rocks like a goat.

Elder's Weekly Review, on April 26, 1905, tells its farmer readers that the type of animal aimed at by all high-class breeders who cater for the army trade is a low-set, compact animal, and not the long-legged, high-standing, short-necked 16 hands animal which almost invariably becomes "a roarer" if turned out to grass, and points out that many horses with silver tubes are to be met with.

The *Register* of October 23, 1905, informs us that in the previous September the South Australian Government received from the High Commissioner of South Africa a despatch requiring about 400 horses for the South African Constabulary, the minimum height to be reduced as regards 20 per cent. of the horses to 14·1

In the "Horse-trainer's Guide," Mr. Digby Collins writes that he had seen many good little horses on almost every racecourse in the kingdom. He recalls the race between Stockwell and Teddington, the one big enough to carry the other, yet the little one had the greatest weight in addition to being a little amiss, and nevertheless defeated his great adversary after perhaps one of the most severe struggles ever witnessed. Mere formation, he states, must be thrown to the winds, and the character of the blood carefully weighed. The breeder must estimate good looks and formation only for just so much as they are worth. The folly of going for looks alone is nothing short of madness. It should always be remembered that, although no animal commands so high a price as the thoroughbred colt of high character, no animal is so valueless if the reverse. Mr. Collins adds that Bay Middleton and the Flying Dutchman have proved decided failures at the stud, yet they were themselves quite unsurpassed as racehorses. In a steeplechase, want of size is no bar to success in the very best company. He says that there are on an average some 1,500 thoroughbred colts and fillies bred every year, out of which there are about three really first-class racehorses, or one in 500, and some twenty or thirty moderate racehorses, or about one in fifty worth keeping in training for the Turf. In maintaining that it is wiser to look to blood than to bigness or beauty, Mr. Collins only repeats what the Arabs have been saying for several thousand years.

In the "Crusades," by T. A. Archer, it is said that the pictures of the time show the Crusaders on low horses, their feet almost touching the ground. Baldwin, King of Jerusalem, is described as mounted on his fleet Arab, and the writer relates that the heavy horses of the Crusaders were no match for the swift-footed Arabs of the Saracens.

In "Egypt," Mr. F. Barham Zincke says a fair horse is seldom more than 14 hands high : he looks too small for a cavalry horse, but it is his great merit to be better than he looks. He is very docile, very hardy, and can go through a great deal of work.

In the "Persian Gulf and South Sea Isles," Sir Edgar Boehm mentions that he passed a lot of Turkish officers mounted on showy little Arabs, and he says that the Arabs are so jealous of their horses that they keep them in the interior at Nejd for fear of the Turks seizing them. Now, as in ancient times, raiders cannot get into the heart of that country.

In "Eclipse and O'Kelley," it is stated that in intelligence and temperament the Celtic pony compares favourably with Arabs. It is usually extremely keen and active, and the skull is like that of a well-bred Arab in its measurements. Naturally, that is so, for this pony has a large infusion of Arab blood.

In "Through Savage Europe," Mr. Harry De Windt writes that at Tikhonitzka the Cossacks mounted their shaggy ponies, which had hitherto wandered freely around the place like human beings, and galloped homewards like the wind. These ponies have been systematically improved by Arab blood.

In "Hazards of Life," Mr. V. Tweedale states that a Gulf Arab is a cross between the big Persian mares and the smaller but far better bred Arab horses.

The *Saltash Gazette* of June 12, 1906, points out that the horses in general in France, Germany and Austria are better than those of England, owing to the free use of Arab blood.

M. Hornez, the administrator of the horse-breeding establishment at Haras, in France, reports that in the year 1905 there were at that place 240 Arabs and 247 thoroughbreds.

Elder's Weekly Review of May 14, 1905, informs its readers than in Basutoland the Government have imported nine pure-bred Arab stallions to improve the native ponies.

The *Australasian* of November 28, 1908, says that England has only just awakened to the fact of her very great deficiency in horses for army purposes, and contrasts the great interest taken in France and in Germany. In the latter country there were 241 thoroughbreds, 100 Arabs, and 220 Anglo-Arabs belonging to the Government.

J. P. Hore, in his "History of Newmarket," says that nearly all the gold and silver coins of the Iceni bear the figure of a horse, and that horse-racing may be traced back to the times of the Romans. He adds that all the successful horses on the Turf from the remotest ages have been of Eastern descent. The earliest mention of horse-races in England, he says, was in the reign of Emperor Severus (A.D. 210), at Netherby, in Yorkshire, and the horses were delicate Arabs of famous speed and stamina. The superiority of the English thoroughbred horse, he continues, is only attributable to the Eastern blood introduced and maintained by the Romans.

The *Mail* of January 1, 1905, points out that the Celt, like the Jew, is an invincible proof of the persistence of race type. That is a fact beyond question, and extends to the Arab horse as well as to the Celt and the Jew.

Dr. Robert Wm. Stewart, in his "Journey in Syria and Palestine," writes that the road over the hill was atrocious, yet the little sure-footed animals got over it without accident.

H. B. Tristram, in the " Land of Israel," states that their horses unhesitatingly " walked up a long flight of steps cut out of the road, which was bare and glossy, without any parapet." His horse slipped, with his haunches overhanging the precipice, where no English horse could have saved itself, but the little animal, after a few struggles with its nose and forefeet, got itself on to the path again. He tells us how his favourite horse, a thoroughbred Arab, with the docility of his race, implicitly followed the commands of the voice, and allowed him to traverse his gun between his ears, and, if he dismounted, would stand patiently till his return or follow at the word of command. He describes two Bedouins splendidly mounted on the finest Arab mares ever seen, with exquisite heads. A party of them pulled up their horses on their haunches within half a spear's length, and, to try their nerves, galloped among the writer and his friends, the spears quivering a few feet from their faces.

In " Mount Omi and Beyond," Mr. Archibald John Little writes that his pony nimbly scrambled over a very difficult place to the safe ground, but a mule immediately behind went rolling down, and was instantly killed. The pony was absurdly small, 11 hands 2 inches, so that he felt some compunction in mounting him until he recollected that he had been loaded daily with 250 pounds of rice and carried his load safely over the steep mountains. The author suggests that these ponies are a survival from Arabs brought into China by the Turkish followers of Genghis Khan, of which there can be little doubt, as for years Arab stallions had been introduced there.

In " The Nile Tributaries of Abyssinia." Sir Samuel Baker relates that he purchased three horses, a bay and two greys, handsome animals, none exceeding $14\frac{1}{2}$ hands, and none had ever been shod, yet their hoofs were as hard as ivory. Abou Do rode a grey mare not exceeding

14 hands, full of fire and speed, which appeared to be able to twist and turn with the suppleness of a snake. Aggahr was an exceedingly fast horse. His gallop was perfection, as easy to himself as to his rider ; there was no necessity to guide him, as he followed an animal like a greyhound, avoiding the trunks of the trees and choosing his route where the branches allowed ample room for the rider to pass beneath. On a pair of rhinoceroses charging, there was no time for more than one look behind. Sir Samuel dug the spurs into Aggahr, and, clasping him round the neck, ducked his head blindly, trusting to Providence and his good horse over big rocks, fallen trees and grass 10 feet high, with the two infernal animals in full chase only a few feet behind him.

In " Patriots and Filibusters," L. Oliphant writes :—

" We learn that the Circassian ponies possessed great pluck and powers of endurance, and in no other country that the author had ever been in do horses perform such extravagant feats. Except in Nepaul, he had never seen such dangerous roads."

In " The River of Golden Sand," Captain Gill mentions that ponies in Northern China are stout, hardy little animals from the Mongolian Plateau, but that they do not come up to the wiry little creatures found in Persia, which are largely Arab. These Mongolian ponies themselves have Arab blood in them. Of the Tibetan ponies he writes that they are docile, and never showed the least sign of temper or vice, and were as hardy as the people themselves. They required no clothing and were scarcely ever groomed. There is little doubt that these ponies have been improved by Arabs.

In " Six Months in Mecca," Mr. J. F. Keane writes that the horses of the Turkish mounted troops are the well-known hardy little Arabs, good horses at their worst, never groomed, and hardly shod. The horses he referred to are doubtless the breed of little Syrian Arabs, spoken of by Stevens in his book, " With Kitchener to Khartoum," sons of Arab horses and not sons of Arab mares. I cannot think it possible that the Turkish Cavalry (except, perhaps, some of the officers) could be mounted on pure Arabs, by reason of the cost.

In " Twenty Years in the Near East," A. H. Bearman narrates how they climbed the Anti-Lebanon, about another 6,000 feet, and thence descended into the Valley of the Baradar, and trotted gaily into Damascus, doing the whole distance of 125 kilometres in about fourteen hours. After a day's stable, his pony took him back just as easily. The mules were slipping in all directions on the huge, slanting, polished slabs of rock, which constituted the path, but the pony scrambled like a cat from bottom to top. From that day onward he never again discarded a horse for a mule on the popular delusion of their superior sure-footedness. The saddle had not been off the pony's back since two o'clock on the preceding afternoon, and he was slightly off his feed that night, but was all right the day after. The ordinary Egyptian mounts, he says, are good little beasts. Doubtless they are mostly Syrian Arabs.

Victor Tissot, in " Unknown Hungary," says that small horses of Barbary origin are found along the Turkish border well-suited to the rugged and rocky countries, and furnishing excellent horses for the cavalry. Some of these horses are certainly of Barbary breed, but more of them from the East.

Lieutenant-General Sir Montagu Gerard, K.C.B., V.C., a wonderful fighter and sportsman, who fought in nearly all our recent great wars, states that one lesson he learned in his campaigning was the great value of the Arab horse. Whilst English and Australian horses got off their feed and rapidly lost condition, the little Arabs would tuck into any species of food, and start fit and fresh in the morning.

He twice shot tigers off a small Arab, and never felt for a moment that there was any particular risk about it. He says that he rode an uncommonly handy and plucky Arab, who swerved at nothing.

General Gerard also says that one little Arab did seventy miles in about twelve hours, and was fit and well at the end of it. Arabs are amenable and tractable as dogs. Their reputation for stumbling he attributes largely to their docility, owing to which they are seldom broken in or taught their paces, but just simply saddled and mounted.

In " The Australian in China," the author tells us that his pony was small, rat-like, and wiry, and carried him without wincing over the stone-flagged pathway, scaling and descending the long flights of steps which led over the mountains.

An article by Thomas F. Dale states that ponies crossed with Arabs will produce small horses of the best riding type — hardy, handsome, enduring and economical; while, as to feed. the Arab horse can work on far less stimulating and expensive food than English horses, which is one reason why Arab blood is so valued on the Continent, where economy is more thought of in horse-keeping than it is in England. The Transvaal War, he says, made a great difference in the prospects of South African horse-breeding ; and by the steady importation of horses, especially of high-class Arabs from the Crabbet Park Stud, endeavours are made to improve the breed.

In " A Varied Life," General E. T. Gordon writes that in the Punjab they forced the enemy to abandon two led horses—one a fine dapple-grey Arab, 14·2 hands, sound in wind and limb, a horse of high quality, and one a steady charger, which carried him well when hog-hunting. The General mentions that he had had a valuable Arab horse cut down by a boar, which appeared to have had the effect of stimulating his love of the dangerous sport after his recovery. He states further that Sheik Mizal delighted him with his stable of Arab horses, which showed great powers of endurance on long journeys and over rough roads. They worked well on scanty fare and the lightest covering at night against cold.

In his "General John Jacob," Mr. Alexander James Shand says that the Beloochees' wiry little ponies, sure-footed as goats, scrambling over rocks and river channels, eluding pursuit, and giving him no little trouble, charged home, and twenty-five of the Beloochees were cut down, but the rest were saved by the fleetness of their horses. These ponies are greatly Arab blood.

Mr. George A. B. Dewar, in "Memoirs of Sir Claude Champion de Crespigny," says that right cleverly the little Arab horses negotiated the ditches.

In "On Foot through Kashmir Valleys," Marion Daughty refers to the hardy, sure-footed hill ponies which the Syces habitually used on the rough tracks, and in which they had such confidence that they even ventured across the rickety swinging bridges, feeling certain that, if there was danger, the ponies would be the first to perceive it.

In "The Land of Ararat," by a Special Correspondent, the author states that at Erzeroum the horses were small, but strong and very steady. They were high-spirited, and well bred, and noted for their great endurance. When parting from his guide, the latter told him that robbers were lying in wait for him behind the hedges. He went with him to the river, and then said : " Now you have an open plain, and your horse is enough for safety. I give you in God's keeping." The guide was satisfied to trust him to the speed and purity of his Arab horse.

In "Tafilet," Mr. W. B. Harris says that almost the sole remainder of the Arab origin of the Berbers of to-day is the fact that they are great horsemen. It is a sight well worth seeing to watch an old ruffian of the tribe galloping about on his handsome desert horse, with a youth holding on to each stirrup and another at the tail. The horses are small, wiry, often very handsome, and capable of standing a great amount of fatigue.

In "Travels in the Three Great Empires of Austria, Russia, and Turkey," C. B. Elliot, F.R.S., observes that the Turkish horses displayed a good deal of blood. "Their horses, not larger than ponies, galloped as fast as we could wish, and faster than ever we had had ever been carried by the heavy horses of Germany."

Mr. J. C. Ewart, in " The English Thoroughbred," says that Napoleon's famous charger was probably a Barb, and that Strabo, writing in the first century, informs us that the Libyan horses, though small, are spirited and so docile as to be guided by a switch.

D. Clarke, in " Travels in Russia, Tartary, and Turkey," remarks that a moderately good Cossack horse will go forty miles at full speed without stopping. But the Circassian horses are of a nobler race of the Arab kind, high-bred, light and small, and the Cossack acknowledges his inability to overtake the Circassian.

Mr. Elliot Warburton, in " The Crescent and the Cross," says that smooth turf or rugged rock seemed all the same to his Arab. He swept eagerly along over hill and hollow, bounding from rock to rock with the ease of a gazelle and the mettle of a bloodhound. The path was so steep and rugged that no English horse with the most cautious guidance could safely travel in it, yet the bold Arabs traverse it at full speed, going at a gallop where it seemed too steep to walk. Once, when day dawned, he found the Arabs had been sleeping under their horses, who had never stirred a limb for fear of hurting them.

In " Algeria," J. R. Morell alludes to Captain Guy de Vernon, of the 8th Chasseurs de Cheval, who recorded that his chasseurs were mounted on horses of native races, supple, skilful, nervous, bold, untiring, and from $13\frac{1}{2}$ to 14 hands high. They would go from 15 to 20 leagues, always on the trot or gallop, without resting and without unbridling. He had known a Morocco horse, mounted by a native trooper, to travel 125 miles in eleven hours without a moist hair or the need of a spur.

He describes Barbary horses as being of a moderate height, head held erect, limbs fine, the pace sure and rapid, and all their movements marked by suppleness and vigour ; never fed except at nightfall, yet it is almost incredible what toils and labour they will go through. The mares of a good breed are beyond all price, and their owners constantly refused to part with them to the French for any consideration.

Mr. Gray Hill, in his book on the Bedouins, speaks of their surefooted little horses, of the well-deserved confidence of their riders, and of the beautiful mare of a sheik who rode her with the most perfect command without the use of bit, stirrups, or girths.

In " Tibet and Nepal," Mr. A. Henry Savage Landor states that the sturdy Tibetan ponies, short, stumpy little brutes, possess most marvellous endurance under circumstances which would kill most horses. They live on whatever grass they can find, which is not much—at best short semi-dried blades, which take a good deal of looking for before you can see them at all. They have all the qualities of a goat and antelope combined. He has seen them with a rider on their back go up gradients where a human being would have great difficulty to go on foot.

Lingi Villari, in " Fire and Sword in the Caucasus," says that his guide was an immensely fat Mingrelian, whose vast proportions made it impossible for him to mount without a step or a heap of stones ; but that, once mounted, he would start off at a gallop down the most difficult tracks. The horses are wiry little mountain ponies, with a distant touch of Arab in them.

In " A King's Hussar, being the Military Memoirs for twenty-five years of a Troop-Sergeant," Major Mole, of the 14th (King's) Hussars, says that most of his time was spent in looking after horses. He had the superintendence of a very considerable number of men and their horses, and had served in each of the three kingdoms, also in India and South Africa, and on sea voyages. On leaving the army he was paraded to receive a silver medal " for long service and good conduct," so his experience was almost unique.

He mentions that the King's celebrated teams of cream-coloured horses, used for State ceremonies and weddings, all entire horses, were so nervous and excitable that, on a summer thunderstorm coming on, every door and window was at once closed, and the gas lit all over the stables, so as to deaden the sound of the thunder and minimize the effects of the lightning flashes. He had been accustomed in India to Persians, Kandaharis, Turkomans, Northern Indians, country breds, with a few Cape horses, and perhaps half a dozen three-parts Arab bred, which were all much smaller and lighter than those we had been accustomed to at home ; but the Arab bred came nearer perfection in symmetry, beauty, and temper than any horses he had ever seen, and they were soon snapped up as chargers by our officers.

The Walers in India were nervous buckjumpers ; they lashed out and jibbed back, and were as frightened as antelopes. It took months to get over this timidity, and in some horses it proved quite incurable. All were more or less addicted to buckjumping. Most of his service was with horses who varied much in disposition. What he writes about the nervousness of the Waler is corroborated by a letter which I recently received from a District Superintendent of Police in India. It is dated March 2, 1911, and tells me that the writer has read my book with pleasure many times ; that he finds it very difficult to get a good staying horse nowadays. The Waler is fast for a few furlongs, but not much good beyond that. He adds that he is very anxious to get a good Arab, and hopes that I can spare him one, or introduce him to some gentleman who can do so.

The author's disquisition on colour may be interesting, as he says their colours gave a very fair idea of their constitutions or characteristics. and what a man of his wonderful experience says is worth noting. Bright chestnuts and light bays he found invariably high-spirited animals, but of nervous, unsettled temperament and delicate constitution. Dark chestnuts and glossy blacks were hardy, and as a rule good tempered.

Rich bays possessed great spirit, but were at the same time docile. Dark greys and iron greys were hardy and of good constitution, whilst light greys were just the reverse. The hardiest and best working horses of all were roans, either strawberry or blue, which were always even-tempered, the easiest to train, and took kindly to everything. They were, in fact, just the opposite to a rusty black, which gains the palm for pig-headedness.

Another curious indication of a horse's character could be gleaned from its white stocking. A horse with one white leg is a bad one, with two white legs " you may sell to a friend," with four white legs you may trust it for a spell, but with three white legs you may safely lay your life on it. So, in effect, says Abd-el-Kadir. I insert this as being exceedingly worthy of note, coming from a clever man of such long and great familiarity with the subject.

Colonel St. Quinton, writing in *Blackwood's Magazine*, November, 1909, considers that polo has been spoiled by the bigger ponies, and is not so good a game, nor does it require nearly so much skill and delicate handling, as the despised old game on smaller ponies, which was much more clever and scientific than you possibly can have it on the high horses now accepted, although the actual pace of the game may be faster.

In " Modern Argentina," W. H. Kochel states that the breeding of polo ponies has been difficult, owing to flukiness. A dam that has thrown an excellent pony may as likely as not, upon a second occasion, produce by the same sire a foal whose stature will eventually exceed the polo limit by a whole hand. This comes about by the parents being cross-breds—not of pure blood—and is owing to mixture of blood.

Edmondo de Amicis, who has travelled great distances in Morocco, and written a most interesting book, interspersed with frequent remarks on the Arab horses he saw, speaks of the American Consul riding a magnificent Arab, and of the beautiful animals ridden by Court officials, merchants, etc. He says that the horses of Morocco are so small that middle-size horses seemed

THE ARAB A LOW HORSE

enormous. In repose and walking they make no show, but put to a gallop they are quite changed and become superb.

At the Polo Ponies Show, in March, 1910, Mr. Tresham Gilbey's Animation was of beautiful quality and delightful manners, and won the Cup. She has a beautiful mouth, and is extraordinarily quick in starting. Mootrub, the well-known chestnut Arab, is the sire. Lady Anne Blunt's Berk, a charming bay, with all the characteristics of the desert-born horse, a beautiful mover, won the First Prize. Animation should draw the attention of breeders to the value of Arab blood. Several other successful and high-priced playing polo ponies are sons of the Arab Mootrub.

I know not what may be the case in England, but I consider that my former book has led to a considerable increase in the number of ponies in use. Certainly, there are more ponies about than there were.

CHAPTER VI

UNIFORM EXCELLENCE OF ARABS, GATHERED FROM VARIOUS AUTHORS

It is very remarkable that continuously all through the ages the pure Arab horse has been praised and celebrated, and that he is so still by all who use him, except only racing gentlemen. This chapter will give the favourable opinions of great numbers of persons, mostly travellers and military men, who have had excellent opportunities of judging, and with a full capacity to judge. It would have been utterly impossible that the Arab horse could have been so greatly and universally praised if he had not deserved it.

Dr. Porter, in " Five Years in Damascus," writes that the road ascended an almost perpendicular cliff by a zigzag route which caused him to despair of the horses being able to find footing; but it seemed but play for them to spring up the rugged stairs. It is startling to a traveller when his steed assumes a vertical attitude, or passes along a precipice brink where a false step would hurl him hundreds of feet below. But experience teaches him to place confidence in his careful Arab, and to ride without fear along paths where an English fox-hunter would deem it madness to risk his neck.

Further on, Dr. Porter mentions that, although in danger of an attack by the Bedouin, and of being plundered, admiration at the Arab horse was the only feeling he entertained. The chief advised him and his party not

EXCELLENCE OF ARABS

to run away, because the raiders' horses were fleet, and our running would give them fresh courage. Dr. Porter was, in fact, not riding the "son of a mare," but only the "son of a horse," and therefore not qualified to compete with the sons of mares of the Bedouins.

In " Persia and its People," Ella G. Sykes writes :—

" When the day's march is over, the traveller will visit the horses, who will neigh softly as he approaches. The Sahib's favourite Arab is very docile, and, when not ridden, trots along with the caravan, and comes like a dog at call. The Arab's most treasured possessions here are beautiful mares as tame and docile as dogs. The mixture of Persian and Arab is delightful to ride, wonderfully sure-footed, and full of spirit and endurance, and gets much attached to its owner, whom it will follow like a dog."

In the " Giant Cities of Basham," the Rev. J. L. Porter mentions that ten or twelve splendidly-mounted Arabs, led by two sheiks also splendidly mounted, came upon them full gallop, their horses leaping from terrace to terrace as lightly as goats across a chasm. He refers again and again to their " noble Arab horses," " a mare of matchless perfection." They rode along a mere goat track, now in a rocky torrent bed, now on the brink of a fearful ravine, now over a slippery crack of naked limestone, now up rude stairs that seemed as if " let down from heaven itself." He says it was a bad and dangerous path, and his nerve was tried when he found one stirrup ringing against the overhanging cliff, while the other was suspended over a fathomless abyss. And yet there are men so ignorant as to say that Arab horses are useless in a hilly country.

Mr. J. P. Hore, in " The History of Newmarket," writes that

" The Duke of Newcastle's horses wanted nothing of being reasonable creatures but speaking, and the Duke said the Barbs were the gentlemen of the horse kind.

He bought several Barbs, among them a grey, the most beautiful horse he ever saw. The Duke recommended a Barb as stallion, which Sir John Fenwick said would get better running horses than the best running horse in England."

In " Heavy Horses," by Herman Biddel and others, it is stated that the Shaddingfield mares had light hearts, wiry legs, and good shoulders, for the pedigree of their sire, Stormer, bred in 1774, takes us back in the direct male line to the Darley Arabian, whence came the indomitable spirit that made this stock famous among the breeders in Suffolk.

From " In a Syrian Saddle," by A. M. Goodrich-Freer (Mrs. H. H. Spoer), we learn that it would have been difficult to find in England any animal with whom you could have carried through one tithe of what their ragged regiment accomplished. The lady was mounted on an Arab capable of running the Derby, and you have to hang on to the precipices there by your eyelids, climb pathless mountains in the dark, descend over solid rock slippery and defenceless, or over shale which disappears beneath your horse's feet, when you may be ten, twelve, or even fourteen hours a day in the saddle. She never once dismounted ; both horse and rider came back as fresh as they started. A native who had ridden sixty hours without dismounting begged permission to join their calvacade.

In " My Journey to Medinah," Mr. John F. T. Keane (All Hajj Mohammud Amin) writes that

" One fellow attacked by three others defended himself with success by dodging and evading their darts by the rapid evolutions of his marvellously-trained horse."

In his book, " On Horseback through Asia," Captain Fred Burnaby writes of a tall dark Circassian mounted on a magnificent coal-black Arab, and of some nice-looking horses standing in his host's room.

EXCELLENCE OF ARABS

Below are a few extracts from a book, published in 1887, by Mr. S. G. W. Benjamin, Minister of the United States to Persia :—

"After a fine display of the mettle of these Arab steeds...."

"... I had to lead, mounted on the noble sorrel Arab I had ridden since my arrival...."

"... Persian horses are every way admirable and possessed of great staying powers...."

"... In the south-west of Persia there is a considerable number of Arabs, and it is to them, doubtless, that Persia is indebted for her very fine breed of Arab horses. The horse of Shiráz, called the Shirazee Arabian, is one of the finest varieties of this noble stock...."

"... The horses used in Persia are invariably stallions; but they are gentle, and accidents with them are rare...."

"... The Persians for thousands of years have reared breeds of horses unsurpassed for excellence; this cannot be entirely the result of accident...."

He describes the cutting of a passage through a snow drift: One of twenty of the best villagers charged the drift at a gallop, and in a second or two nothing could be seen but the head of the rider, his steed entirely hidden. He then backed the animal out. The next horseman rode at the place, and each Kurd followed in succession till finally they forced a passage.

In "Our ride through Asia Minor," Mrs. Scott Stevenson says that Djeinel Pasha had some very fine Arab horses, and she was astonished at the prices paid, in some cases as much as two or three hundred pounds. She continues:

"The path is very rugged, but the horses got on famously, gathering their four feet close together on a ledge of rock, springing lightly across a chasm, scrambling laboriously up a slippery incline, and picking their steps one by one as they wound around corners so sharply that the slightest mistake would have sent them crashing to the bottom."

In "Princes of India," Sullivan relates that Timour marched 100 miles from Adjodin to Ballingi in one day, and on September 5, 1393, he marched eighty miles without a halt, swam the Tigris, and took Baghdad ; and that the Turkomans have been known to march 1,000 miles in ten consecutive days.

In "Persia, the Land of the Imauns," Basset tells how he had to ride a horse, just from a journey of nine parasangs, a distance of nearly seventy-two miles. The King's stables, he says, contained some very fine Arab and Turkoman horses. The Turkoman has great powers of endurance, and he considers the Arab Turkoman and Persian breeds among the best horses in the world.

In his "Ride in Morocco," Francis Macnabb remarks that the horses appeared three-parts thoroughbred. He never met with one which had any faults or ill-temper. They would walk all day without food, and their constitution was the hardest in the world. They would eat anything except prickly pears and aloes. He draws particular attention to Abd-el-Kadir's magnificent bay charger.

This horse, Conrad, created quite a sensation even there, and a dozen hands were stretched out to pat him. He also mentions a very fine horse of the pure Abda breed.

In his book, "The Spell of Egypt," published in 1910, Mr. Robert Hitchens only refers twice to the horse ; on the first occasion he writes of a Bedouin's quickly-stepping horse, and on the second he says :—

"If you have ever ridden an Arab horse to the verge of the great desert, you will remember the bound thrilling with fiery animation which he gives when he sets his feet on the sand."

Walter Keating Kelley, the author of "In Syria and the Holy Land," was particularly struck with the fine shape of the "trusty horses."

"The Bedouin and his horse should be seen together, for they make a noble figure. When the rider is on the

EXCELLENCE OF ARABS

ground the horse stands by with his tail drooping and his head down. But, when the Bedouin springs into the saddle, an electric energy seems breathed into man and horse; the rider utters a yell, and the horse bounds forth and makes the air whistle with his speed."

Numerous writers have referred to this.

These horses, one says, may be trusted with safety on the worst roads, and their gentle spirit, hardness and intelligence endear them to the traveller, while their powers of endurance are most remarkable. He quotes Colonel Napier, who had an old grey horse that on more than one occasion carried him for sixteen or eighteen hours at a stretch without food, and once cantered from Hebron to Jaffa, nearly fifty miles, without pulling. He adds that at the end of such journeys Arab horses get only a few handsfull of barley, no bedding, no grooming, and that generally the saddle is never removed. Like all other authorities he is struck with the surefootedness and remarkable sagacity of the animals.

Baron von Taubenhein, equerry to the King of Wurtemburg, made a long tour in Syria and the desert in the year 1840 expressly for the purpose of procuring brood mares and stallions for the royal stud. His authority on horseflesh is not to be disputed, and he dilates in a letter to a friend on the excellent hired horses of Syria.

In "The Gates of India," Sir Thomas Holdich says that Alexander's victories were won by the sweeping and resistless force of his cavalry charges. . . . He can only regard with astonishment Ferrier's record of a ride from "Tarsi" (Parsi) to Herat, at least ninety miles, in one night. . . . He had been an Anglo-maniac, and no one so highly prized the splendid action of the English horse as he did, but henceforth he set the Arab horse above every other, and he adds that he speaks from experience of his extraordinary performances. I give his own words:

"I have journeyed all over Lebanon, Anti-Lebanon, and part of the desert, on a hired Arab mare eighteen years old and scarcely $12\frac{1}{2}$ hands high, and I do not remember ever to have been so thankful to any horse for its good service as I was to this. You can have no conception of the character of the roads in Lebanon. It is an incessant clambering over rocks, on which the horse has to mount or descend 2 or 3 feet at a step; the track is sometimes strewed with loose rolling stones, sometimes it runs jaggedly and unevenly along the verge of a precipice. Marshy places, too, are not infrequent, through which the horse, sinking almost to its belly, has to labour for half an hour long, yet over such roads as these it goes on without lagging from six in the morning till eight in the evening; and I can assert that I could not in the very last quarter of an hour discover the least abatement of strength or spirit in the animal I rode. For many days I never, in the most literal sense of the words, took hold of the reins."

His party visited the Emir's splendid Arabians, and he remarks that it is only in such stables or at the door of the tent with the Arabs of the desert that a just idea can be formed of the Arabian horse.

In an appendix to " An Overland Trek from India," by Edith Fraser Benn, her husband writes:

" The chestnut Arab, Commandant, which carried me on the first part of my journey from Quetta to Seistan, has now eclipsed that performance by carrying not only myself, but the greater part of my kit as well, at the average rate of a little over forty-eight miles a day for ten consecutive days."

I fancy from my reading that the roads there are terrible.

He describes the horses looking at them with inquisitive attention owing to their European costumes, but their shyness soon wore off and they came gracefully forward and yielded their necks to be patted and caressed. The varied expression possessed by these horses is not to be believed by those who have not witnessed it. He admired immensely several priceless mares, and made an offer of 10,000 piastres for one of them; but no temptation would induce an Arab to part with a mare of pure breed, and he could purchase nothing.

EXCELLENCE OF ARABS

In " The Passing of the Shereefian Empire," E. Ashmead-Bartlett says that he was singularly fortunate in acquiring a splendid Algerian barb stallion, six years old, very strong and fast, and a first-rate jumper. He considered it the best animal he ever owned in any campaign, and he proceeds :

" On my return to England it was very sad to have to part with him. . . . Nothing could disturb the peaceful equanimity of his temperament, and he would allow you to use his neck as a pillow at any time without making the least effort to rise. . . . A more comfortable animal to ride on a long day's outing I have never known, and I have always regretted not having been able to bring him back to England."

It is Keating Kelly, I think, who quotes a story by Lamartine, where a wounded Arab prisoner had his legs bound ; but his horse gnawed the cord which bound him. Lamartine's story may not be quite accurately stated, but it shows how deeply seated is the tradition as to the grand qualities of the Arab.

Schomberg, in his " Travels in India and Kashmir," mentions that all the horses which he saw at the royal stables were of Arabian or Persian blood. Some were of extreme beauty, and excited his warmest admiration, especially a white one, and a bay. They were, without exception, of medium size.

Edward Gibbon and Simon Oakley, in their book on " The Saracens : their Rise and Fall," maintain that Arabia is the genuine and original country of the horse. There is doubtless much to support this view.

It is recorded that Abu-Obeidah willingly paid twice as much for pure Arabs as for other horses, owing to their superior quality ; and Sir John Mandeville, in his " Book of Travels," mentions that it was customary for the Tartars to present their Emperor with a white horse. He alludes also to the practice of the Tartars to simulate flight, and then to shoot from behind as they are fleeing.

Walter B. Harris, in his "Travels in Morocco" (1889), describes the charging, saluting, firing, stopping short, and other wonderful feats in horsemanship, such as turning when riding at full speed and shooting directly behind.

Dr. Barth, in his "Travels in North Africa," refers to the excellent and very handsome breed of horses, which bear fatigue "marvellously." He says that his own horse carried him during three years of almost incessant hard work, and speaks of his exalted feeling when mounted on his "noble charger."

His mare was known over the whole desert as Bint-el-Nejineh, and never lay down even after the longest day. He says: "Dear old Bint! Many a stretching gallop did I have on her."

Dr. Eugene Schuyler says that in Turkestan the Kirghiz will sometimes ride over one or two hundred miles to some function, such as a marriage, where races, often over twelve, fifteen, or twenty miles, are the main feature of the feast. The horses are wiry and enduring, and show truly wonderful qualities in these long races. At Orenburg he saw one race when thirteen miles were run in twenty-nine minutes and thirty seconds.

He adds that the Turkoman horses are of purer breed and more like the Arab than the Kirghiz, and capable of undergoing any amount of fatigue and hardship.

Mr. J. F. Fraser, in his "Pictures from the Balkans," mentions that he had an escort of fine horses, with more than a touch of Arab blood, and no man could have been closer friends of the Turkish soldiers than their horses. Whenever there was a halt and the soldier rested, his horse was close to him, having his nose patted and being talked to.

Field-Marshal Sir Evelyn Wood, in the Indian Mutiny, bought a short-backed, well-bred chestnut Arab for £110, which was, he says, the cheapest horse he ever possessed. In eleven months he carried him nearly 5,000 miles. They named him "the Pig," for he would eat any food within

EXCELLENCE OF ARABS

reach, from milk out of a saucer to raspberry jam. He was fast, and once, when chased by Gwalior horsemen, after fleeing 300 yards through the jungle, they came on prickly growth two feet high, which all the others turned to avoid ; but, as the Gwalior horsemen were too close, he drove his horse at it, and he went over it or through it in a few bounds. He never underwent such continuous fatigue as once when riding " the Pig " he lost the holding-power of his legs, having been eighty hours without sleep. He had nearly arrived at the limit of human endurance. . . . The Arab squadron outlasted all others. " The Pig " lay down one day when Sir Evelyn dismounted, but he ate his food greedily without offering to rise. On one occasion, as the outpost reports showed, he passed from post to post in a continuous ride of thirty-six hours, covering 110 miles. It really makes one ashamed of one's countrymen when they scoff at a statement like this by a man like Sir Evelyn Wood.

Mr. Gilbert Watson, in " The Voice of the South," describes an Arab stallion, which stood arching his neck, and flicking at the flies with his long tail, his nostrils dilated, his coat shining in the sun, and beautiful as a picture. The Cadi had purchased him when a foal, and was greatly attached to him.

Mr. G. W. Forrest, C.I.E., in " Sepoy Generals," says that General Wellesley, after the Battle of Assaye, wrote General Malcolm to let him have " the grey Arab."

Mr. Francis MacCullagh, in his book, " With the Cossacks," writing of the cavalry used in Mischenko's celebrated raid, speaks of the Caucasians on their graceful Arab horses. One young colonel rode a horse almost worth its weight in gold.

Mr. Walter K. Kelly, in his " History of Russia," states that the Russians could not keep their ground against the Tartar cavalry, as the Tartars had the finest horses.

In " Ponies," in 1906, Mr. John Hill states that Colonel Henriques was particularly fond of the Arab, both pure and as a cross, for polo ponies. The great success of the famous Mootrub at the stud is a proof that the Colonel was right.

Mr. A. Trevor-Battye, in "A Northern Highway of the Tsar," 1897, says that no clothing is ever put on a North-Russian horse. After coming in steaming hot, he stands outside in the bitter wind and snow till morning, without suffering from chill or inflammation.

In "Arabia, Egypt, and India," Mrs. Isabel Burton states that at Lipizza, in Hungary, Arab stallions are crossed with Hungarian, Croat, and sometimes English mares; that at Bombay, at Ali Abdullah's stables, she saw some perfect colts, which he had by horses imported from Persia, Syria, and the breeding districts of Turkish Arabia. Sir Salar Jung lent her a beautiful grey Arab, large, powerful and showy. He had never before had a side-saddle on, but did not seem to mind it a bit.

Budgett Meakin, in "Life in Morocco," says that, as in the days of yore, the Arabs excel to-day in performing the most dexterous feats on horseback at full gallop, tossing their guns in the air, whirling round their firearms without stopping, swinging their long weapons underneath their horses, and seizing them upon the other side. The studs of the Oel Nogli in the vicinity of Bussora, the author says, are valued at 8,000 piastres a mare (about £660); one sold at Acre for 15,000 piastres (£1,250). Colonel Hamilton Smith is quoted as stating that there was a bet against time, in which an Arab horse at Bangalore, in the Presidency of Madras, ran 400 miles in four consecutive days in July, 1840. The same officer gives a still more striking instance of speed and endurance, when Aga Bahram's Arab carried his rider from Shiranz to Teheran (522 miles) in six days, remaining three to rest, and then went back in five, after which he remained nine at Shiranz, and then returned again to Teheran in seven.

Another horse of the Aga's carried him from Teheran to Koom, eighty-four miles, starting at dawn in the morning,

EXCELLENCE OF ARABS

and arriving two hours before sunset. Reference is made to the Turkoman horse as deriving its beauty and good qualities from the Arab, and to all breeds in Persia more or less crossed with the Arab, as having great sureness of foot and extraordinary power of endurance. He then expatiates on the excellence of the Spanish horses by reason of the Phœnician settlements there and the Carthaginians in their invasion introducing magnificent steeds of Numidian, Libyan, and African Arabs.

Mr. Philip H. M. Wynter, in " The Queen's Errands," describes crossing the desert to Suez with a good pair of mules for wheelers and entire Arabs for leaders.

Sir A. Henry Layard, in his " Autobiography and Letters," says that the Vladika possessed a beautiful Arab, a present from the Pasha of Bosnia. He tells us that in Bulgaria they had to cross precipitous mountains by a difficult bridle-path, and were twenty-two hours in the saddle. He had three strong sturdy horses, although small, accustomed to long journeys and little provender and to carry heavy loads, and when amongst the Turkomans their guide had to hold his horse by the tail to prevent it slipping down the polished rocks or falling over the precipice.

Lieutenant-Colonel Stuart, in " Residence in Persia," speaks of the beautiful chargers. " Ellis rode a horse of Turkoman breed, valued at £250. Sir H. Bethune left a large stud to be sold, amongst them three beautiful Arabs, valued at £500 each."

In " Walks in Algiers," G. Leguin states that some of the horses are very beautiful, and that Abd-el-Kadër was mounted on a magnificent black charger, sometimes making it spring with all four legs in the air, and sometimes walking for some yards on its hind legs. At Blidah there is a stud of stallions (*Dépôt de Rémonte*), among which are some beautiful Arab and Syrian horses.

So long ago as A.D. 1566, Thomas Bludeville mentions the Turk, the Barbarian, the Sardinian, the Neapolitan, the Jennet of Spain, the Hungarian—all of which were Arabs or nearly Arabs—as amongst the most worthy breeds of horses.

In "A Tropical Dependency," Lady Lugard tells us that in Timbuctoo, amongst the possessions of the rich, good horses would seem to have been the most valued, and horses from Barbary would always fetch their price.

In "Egypt, Palestine, and Phœnicia," F. Bouet states that he had never seen in Malta any but handsome, well-bred horses, even those employed in the most ordinary and laborious kinds of work. In Egypt he saw splendid horses. In Samaria he describes the riders as being asleep by the side of their horses, some of which were very fine. One white mare from Nejd was especially lovely.

In "Recollections of My Life," Sir Joseph Fayrer says that the King of Oudh sent him a young Arab horse, which turned out a great beauty. He kept him all through the siege, and speaks of him as "my gallant little Arab." He adds that the Arab is the best cavalry horse of his inches in the world, which is perhaps the reason why Arab horses find a much better market on the Continent than in England. The French and German soldiers desire, he says, a first-rate troop-horse; they do not want a leggy roarer, half as high as a church tower.

Mr. Thomas F. Dale, author of "Riding, Driving, and Kindred Sports," says that

"The reason why foreign cavalry is so much better mounted than our own, which is the worst horsed in Europe, is because foreign Governments breed from Arabs, for the Arab horse is the ideal thoroughbred of the world, and he will eat and drink anything, as everyone who has taken these horses on long journeys or on service will know."

Mr. Dale refers to the strong motives an Arab has for keeping the blood of his horse pure—in fact, his life, for one thing, depends upon it.

EXCELLENCE OF ARABS

Mr. Dale continues that the record of the best Arab strains has been kept in so trustworthy a manner that from long before the days of the Prophet the Arab horse has been bred closely to acknowledged strains until he has become the most thoroughbred horse in the world. One proof of this is that he is without exception the most prepotent of sires. Arab blood, once introduced, is sure to reappear. Mr. Dale sees the Arab type reappear in the Highland, New Forest, and Exmoor ponies; in hunters in the field; in hackneys; in harness horses, and among race-horses in the paddock. We owe to the Arabs a great debt for preserving the priceless blood so pure as they have done. Like our own native ponies, the Arab is of more value for the qualities he transmits than for those he has as an individual. Only the Arab horses can infuse that quintessence of equine generosity, sweetness, and courage, which make the horse most available for work, for sport, or for war.

He says that the readiness of resource shown in the kick back of the Irish hunter at a bank came from Arab ancestors. The Arab is the foundation head of blood stock all over the world, and there should continue to be an inflow of that blood into our horse-breeding stocks, which is advantageous to hunters, indispensable to the horses of our Indian possessions, and, indeed, to all horses of the British Empire. A first-rate Arab is most pleasant when other horses begin to tire; he is full of life when they are hanging on your hand. Mr. Blunt's horses are all of undeniable pedigree, and of typical make and shape.

Mr. Dale maintains that the Arab cross has not been properly estimated in England, partly because other horses often obtain the credit due to his influence, and partly because he has seldom had a fair trial by the introduction of horses of true and undoubted pedigree. In addition to those causes there are two others: the disinclination of Englishmen to try new methods and the exaggerated liking for big horses. It is curious that the very men who advocate large horses should condemn big hounds. Experience teaches us that the small horse is the best for work. He recovers sooner from fatigue, is generally sounder, and of all small horses the Arab is the king. Of the many Arabians that have been imported, the Crabbet horses are those of which we can say that they are of undoubted pedigree. Almost all horse-breeders, except English ones, have found out the value of the pure-bred Arab. Crabbet has exported to Russia, to Austria, and to France, where the influence of the Arab as the best light cavalry horse in the world is much valued in the breeding of troop-horses. South Africa, Australia, South America have all benefited largely by the importation of Arab blood, and the demand in South Africa is steadily increasing. The Arab cross is being used with success also in the West Indies, Java, and other parts of the tropics, where the English thoroughbred cross is useless. In polo-pony breeding the Arab strain has been invaluable. The Marwari and Kathiawari horses of India show considerable signs of Arab blood, and offer another instance of the truth that Arab blood can be developed in any direction desired. Some of the very best horses for cavalry in India are bred at Junagarh by crossing an Arab with selected Kathiawar mares. Walers are cheaper and can go faster than Arabs, but it seems to him the old style of hog-hunting with a gallant Arab was better.

In " Eclipse and O'Kelly," the author says that

" The horses used for breeding by the Arazah tribes are not chosen for size and shape, or for any quality of speed or stoutness, but only for their blood. Tommy Atkins is a grand fellow, the saving of the nation, always to be honoured and relied on to the last; but he will follow blood in a little man to the death with all his heart when he will despise a Goliath of coarser fibre."

The author is also of opinion that the blood of the Darley Arabian proved so potent because he was a pure representative of the oldest and best indigenous breed of horses in the world. He says that the Arabian was the original type from which both the Barb and the Turk were only derivatives, and it was from the East, and not

EXCELLENCE OF ARABS

from the West, that Ancient Egypt took the best breed, which supports Mr. Blunt, and differs from Professor Ridgeway.

He states, further, that the horse of the Nejd may be called indigenous. It is different from every other breed, has preserved its excellencies longer, and has had more influence in the improvement of horses all over the world than any other. The primeval horse left behind in Central Asia typified by Prejvalsky's horse is a coarser breed, which furnished the aboriginal stock of Europe, improved by successive importations of Eastern horses. The indigenous Arabian horse of Nejd suggests many a century before the Koran was written. It was the Southern blood in his best horses which gave William the Conqueror his victorious cavalry at Hastings.

He goes on to say that an unvarying tradition and accurate, artistic presentments throughout the centuries show the excellence of the original Keheilan, of which the Darley Arabian was one. The exact type still persists in Lord Roberts' famous charger and in Mr. Blunt's pastures at Crabbet Park. It is easier to imagine what the typical pure breed of the Arab was than is the case with any other animal, as its points are so prepotent throughout the record of its life-history.

W. G. Fogg, in "Arabistan," writes of a private carriage drawn by a pair of handsome Arabian horses, and says that the Syrian horses were sure-footed, intelligent animals. The party stopped to admire a beautiful iron-grey Arab mare. Her arched neck, delicate nostrils, intelligent eyes, and smooth limbs would have turned the head of a horse-fancier. A Bedouin never parts with such an animal, and if she dies the whole tribe goes into mourning. Some of the famous Nejdean breed in the royal stables at Raidah were the loveliest horses that the author had ever seen or imagined: of exquisite elegance, with most intelligent and singularly gentle looks, and legs as if made of hammered iron. He also speaks of a full-blooded Arab which he had seen the day before scouring over the plain like wind.

In "Nineveh and its Remains," Mr. Layard relates that Ali Effendi, chief of the Mosul branch, was mounted on a well-known white Arab, beautiful in form, and pure in blood, but of great age; and describes the horseman's galloping and other feats, as mentioned by several other authorities quoted in this book. A young chestnut mare belonging to the Sheik was one of the most beautiful creatures he ever beheld, with the lightness and elegance of the gazelle. The party involuntarily stopped to gaze at her. Lofuk was the owner of a mare of matchless beauty, on which Mohammed Emin, Sheik of the Jebours, assured Mr. Layard that he had seen Lofuk ride down the wild ass. Lofuk esteemed her above all the riches of the tribe, and for her he would have forfeited all his wealth.

In his "Russian Campaign against the Turkomans," Charles Marvin says that the Tekke horse is peerless to race at full speed for ten or fifteen miles at a stretch. To proceed at a gallop—the usual riding pace of the Turkomans—110 miles a day for several days in succession is a very common thing. The Persians and the Kurds often give 1,200 roubles (£150) for a Tekke thoroughbred. This breed descends from a cross between the Persian horse and 450 Arab mares, which Tamerlane (one of the world's mightiest conquerors) caused to be brought from Arabia to improve the Turkoman stock.

The Cossacks, he says, were splendidly mounted on Turkoman horses, but the Tekkes were mounted on swifter horses, and the Russian cavalry was inferior to the Turkoman, and still more so to the Tekkes, whose horses excited the admiration of all who saw them.

The World's Work, March, 1911, states that

"France boasts of only 125 Arab stallions, but their importance is considerable, for they give to their gets sobriety, endurance, character, and courage. . . . Thirty thousand Anglo-Arabs are foaled every year, and they are excellent either for saddle or light harness. The Anglo-Arab is easily kept in condition, is a good galloper, a good hunter, and the officers say he is the very best for light artillery. Anglo-Arabs are really the saddle-horses of the nation, and the breeding of these is fostered by racing societies and by the Ministers of Agriculture and of War."

In " The Game of Polo," Mr. Thomas F. Dale says:

" Eastern ponies are good in proportion as they approach the high-class Arab, and we must judge the Eastern pony by what he is rather than what he looks. Many players will get more fun out of good Arabs than inferior English or Irish ones. The Arab is sound, hardy, of good constitution, but does not go so well as a rule on soft ground, as he likes to hear his feet rattle. He is easy to play, and learns the game rapidly, and is a bold and rather clever hustler. The clever way in which he will avoid one heavier than himself, and will shoulder another off in a close struggle, is worth seeing.

" Arabs have been used with varying success, but it should be borne in mind that many Arabs in this country are really cross-bred animals of uncertain origin and pedigree, and we know as a general rule that mongrels do not make useful sires. The best small pony in the world is the Burinesa, which is largely Arab."

Mr. Eliot Warburton, in " The Crescent and the Cross," travelling in Syria, speaks of " galloping on a spirited little Barb "; of being " mounted on a fine horse owned by the Sheik "; and being " mounted on a gallant Barb, sweeping across the desert." He tells of a Bedouin splendidly mounted, and of the proud carriage of his horse. He describes his untiring Arab. It was always fresh and as vigorous as when he started. On one occasion he had been just twenty-five hours in the saddle from the time he mounted him the preceding day. In one place he descended a steep path that would have puzzled a European goat; at another the road wound sometimes along a deep ravine, sometimes over a mountain's brow, and was " nothing but a steep and rocky path along which in England a goat alone could be expected to travel." Their horses, however, went along it at a canter, though the precipice sometimes yawned beneath their outside stirrup.

He writes that he cannot repress his love and admiration of the Arab horse, in which the pride and power of the Arabs lie. They are noble animals, he says; no less remarkable for their chivalrous disposition than for their strength and endurance; gallant, yet docile; fiery, and yet gentle; full of mettle, yet patient as a camel. They are very ferocious towards each other, but suffer the little children to pull them about and play with them.

The head is beautiful; the expansive forehead, the brilliant prominent eye, and the delicately-shaped ear, would testify to nobleness in any animal. The withers high, and the shoulders well thrown back; the fine, clean limbs, with their bunches of startling muscle; and the silken skin, beneath which all the veins are visible, show proofs of blood that never can deceive.

The author states that a friend rode his horse from Cairo to Suez, eighty-five miles, in twelve hours; then rested twelve, and returned within the following twelve. During these journeys the horse had no refreshments except a gulp of water once to cool the bit. He assures us that he had been on the same horse twenty-four hours on one occasion, and for upwards of thirty on another, without any rest or refreshments except once for a half an hour, when a few handfuls of barley were the only food. In both of these cases the horses never tasted water throughout their journeys. Some of his young friends used to ride the same horses at a gallop almost the whole distance—about sixty miles—to Djoun and back over roads that would appear impossible for an English horse to climb. He mentions these instances as of daily occurrence. The horse of the true Nejd breed will gallop, they say, 125 miles without drawing a thick breath.

The choicest horses come from the remoter parts of the desert, and cannot be said to have a price, as nothing but the direst necessity will induce their owners to part with them. The Kochlan Arabs are extremely scarce.

EXCELLENCE OF ARABS

I never saw an exception to their docility, high spirit, or endurance even among the hacks of Beyrout and Jerusalem.

In "Travels in the Steppes of the Caspian Sea," M. Xavier H. D. Hell writes:

"Their manœuvres surpass everything a European can imagine—furious gallops, grace, impetuosity of movement—displaying inimitable address, and concluding with a general mêlée which terrified not a few spectators, while discharges of musketry and neighing of horses completed the illusion."

The horses were excellent, strong, agile, and of great endurance. The author often rode a Kalmuck horse eighteen and even twenty-five leagues without once dismounting. These horses are small, but of astonishing spirit and bottom. It has often been ascertained by the Imperial garrisons that Circassian marauders have got over twenty-five or even thirty leagues of ground in a night.

In "The Land of the Lion and Sun," C. J. Wells says that Pierson, with wet eyes, told him of the death of his horse: a 14-hands pure-bred Arab, with a large scar of a spear-wound a foot long on his shoulder, otherwise perfect, of angelic temper, but small, as all Arabs are. His muzzle almost touched his chest as he arched his neck, and his action was very high, yet easy. He seemed an aristocrat compared to the rest. His thin and fine mane and tail were like silk. He had a chestnut Arab ten years, which never had to be struck or spurred. A pressure of the knee and a shake of the rein would make him fly to his utmost. He was fast, and, small as he was, he carried his 12 stone comfortably. As a ladies' horse he was perfect, having a beautiful mouth, while he followed like a dog, and nothing startled him or made him shy.

He states that the horses of North Persia are the Turkoman, and are tall, ungainly animals, sometimes over 16 hands, but they will get over 100 miles a day at a jog or loose canter, and will keep it up for ten days. They have been constantly crossed with Arabs, the Gulf Arabs, so-called because they are shipped from the Persian Gulf and are the result of cross-breeding from Persian mares with the smaller and better-bred Arab.

" They are quite free from vice, fast, and with most of the good points of the Arab. They have magnificent shoulders, and are full of bottom, always full of spirit, and willing, their faults being that they are little, delicate, and dainty feeders. They are very surefooted, going full speed over the roughest ground or loose stones. The real Arabs are too well known to need description, and are all that the heart could desire, save as to size. They stand 13·2 to 14·2 hands, seldom more, and cost from 500 kerans up to anything."

The author was ordered to Fasa—ninety miles from Shiraz—and started on a little bay pony, which he did not think could possibly carry him; but he went off at a canter, and arrived at Fasa under the stipulated time, the pony seemingly not at all distressed.

In " Travels in the East," P. R. Madden says of Arab horses :

" They never lie down, night or day. A real Arab horse is worth from £300 to £500. They are so free from vice that it is common to see the Bedouin children playing under their bellies."

The author had ten or a dozen pure mares in a paddock who used to come down to the manager's children and surround them, and take bits of grass from their hands, and not one of the children was ever hurt.

Admiral Sir Henry Keppel, who had great experience of horses, in his " Sailor's Life," says that during the Crimean War, Omar Pasha, almost certainly the greatest General in Europe, mounted him on his (Omar's) favourite charger, an Arab, and that he never saw so beautiful an animal.

The celebrated traveller, Madam Ida Pfeiffer, in her " Visit to the Holy Land," noticed

" The horse on which the Sultan rode as of rare beauty, a true Arabian. The Emperor's State horses were splendid creatures, the majority of true Arabian breed. Their spirited appearance and beautiful pace excited the admiration of all. The Arab horses at first sight looked anything but handsome, but, when mounted, they became transformed, lifting their small graceful heads with their fiery eyes. They threw out their slender feet with matchless swiftness, and bounded away over stock and stone with a step light and yet secure. It was quite a treat to see the horses exercise, and they were compelled to labour unceasingly from sunrise until evening without ever receiving a feed during the day's journey. The Arabian horse is the only one capable of enduring so much hardship."

She describes the fearful dizzy road as a flight of stone stairs upon which their good Syrian horses carried them in perfect safety both upwards and downwards.

In " Recollections of Siberia," C. H. Cottrell mentions that he was told by a General of Cossacks that, if only Cossack horses had been used instead of camels, the Russians might have reached Khiva in their attack, which failed.

Mrs. G. A. Rogers, in " Winter in Algeria," says that the French officers in Algiers had beautiful horses. One beautiful bay Arab was perfect in all its paces, full of life, yet very gentle. The half-stupid looks which Arab steeds usually put on before starting vanish the instant they are put to their speed.

Mrs. F. B. Workman and William Hunter Workman in their book, " Algerian Memories," tell of an Arab horseman inclined to try the mettle of his horse against their wheels. They accepted the challenge, and attained a velocity that no horseman could safely exceed on a descending grade, leaving him behind ; but, when the level was reached, in a twinkling he flew by them like a whirlwind, and they were led to shout "Well done!" as he passed.

In Bannister's "Survey of the Holy Land," it is stated that "the horses of the East, especially the beautiful breed of Arabia, are proverbial for their sagacity and attachment to their owners."

Zenaide A. Rogozin mentions "In Chaldea" robber tribes of Bedouins from the adjoining Arabian deserts, mounted on their matchless horses, who cross the border with a facility dreaded by travellers. In another place he speaks of their wonderful priceless horses, who are to them as their own children.

In the "Country of the Moors," Edward Rae says that the horse he rode was the Kaid's, a splendid iron grey, a Barb, so powerful and spirited that he felt that he could have fled with him to the desert whenever he pleased.

Count Henry Krasinski, in his "Cossacks of the Ukraine," says that the horses of the Don are small, but extremely vigorous, and proof against all kinds of fatigue. They clear all difficulties of the ground, carry their riders everywhere with facility, and are content with the most meagre fare. He remembered having seen a Persian stallion as white as snow, except his mane and tail, which were as black as coal, that excited the admiration of everybody, and was purchased at a high price.

In "Eastern Persia," Major-General Sir F. J. Goldsmith tells how Zohrab Khan met them with a dozen horsemen, who went through the usual feats with their horses at a gallop.

In "The Blue Ribbon of the Turf," L. H. Curzon says that Mr. Singleton, trainer to Mr. Wilberforce Read, had to come to the conclusion that English horses might be greatly improved by the infusion of a dash of Arab blood, and strongly advised his master to put one of his mares to such a horse.

EXCELLENCE OF ARABS

In "Mohammed and the Rise of Islam," Professor Margoliouth, the author, says that the fortresses of the Mohammedans were the backs of their horses, which were of the noblest.

In "The History of the Mogul," T. F. Catron says the Empire had a prodigious number of horses bought from Persia, Arabia and Tartary. Those which are bred in India are weak and washy.

In "Nineveh and its Remains," R. Layard says that Schloss and his horsemen galloped round them, bringing the ends of their lances into such a proximity with his body that, had the mares refused to fall instantaneously back on their haunches, or had they stumbled, he would have been transfixed.

William Kaye, in his "Life of Lord Metcalfe," says that General Smith's cavalry, in order to attack Ameer Khan, pushed across the Doab, taking little account of distance or fatigue, and that their horses seemed to be sustained by the spirit and impelled by the enthusiasm of the riders.

In "Across Coveted Lands," A. Henry Savage Landor states that the Persian post-horse is a most wonderful animal. Its endurance and powers of recovery are extraordinary. He rode a magnificent stallion presented by the Sultan.

In "From the Niger to the Nile," G. Boyd Alexander mentions that the Tubus have small ponies, on which they are accustomed to travel very great distances, concentrating quickly, and scattering as suddenly. These ponies are of Eastern origin, and closely resemble the Berbers in type. They come from North and East, and are willing goers. Vicious horses are rare. In other words, they have much Arab blood in them.

In "Hindustan under Free-Lances," H. G. Keene states that Thomas, the celebrated free-lance adventurer, mounted on a fine Persian horse, burst out and drove off a party of the enemy who tried to intercept him. His horse carried him 120 miles in twenty-four hours. It lived for long afterwards in the stable of Sir F. Hamilton, the British Resident at Benares.

In "Persia Revisited" (1895), General Sir T. E. Gordon, K.C.I.E., says that the ordinary Persian horses are small, but very wiry and endurable, capable of very long journeys. The stables of the Shah contain the very best blood in Asia, and comprise the pick of the finest horses in Arabia and Persia.

The Prince pointed out to him a well-shaped grey Arab, the last winner of the nine-miles race in twenty-five minutes. The late Shah had not a single English or European riding-horse in his stables. He had a high appreciation of Arab and Eastern horses, and found it difficult to understand what he considered the fancy prices paid in England for racing stock. The winner of the 20 miles race did it in 48 minutes 45 seconds, while a race over $13\frac{1}{2}$ miles was done in 27 minutes 30 seconds.

Of nineteen races run over this course, the average time was 33 minutes 40 seconds.

Dr. Scharff, author of "The Irish Horse and its Early History," stated in *Nature*, February 11, 1909, that the modern Irish horse shows remarkable traces of an Eastern strain, currently believed to be due to the introduction of Spanish horses. Irish hunters are now much better than the English.

In "The Land of the Blessed Virgin," Mr. W. S. Maugham says that

"Agnador, snorting with pleasure, cantered over the uneven ground, nimbly avoiding holes and deep ruts with the surefootedness of his Arab blood. An Andalusian horse cares nothing for the ground on which he goes, though it be hard and unyielding as iron, and he clambers up and down steep rocky precipices as happily as he trots along a cinder-path."

The mare he rode was really magnificent, holding her head beautifully. She carried the heavy Spanish saddle as if it were nothing.

EXCELLENCE OF ARABS

In " A Syrian Saddle," A. Goodrich-Freer says

" It would have been difficult to find in England any animal with whom you could have carried through one tithe of what our ragged regiment accomplished. Our two grooms had the management of eight animals under conditions which seemed especially designed for their destruction, where there was not a blade of grass, and perhaps for a whole day not a drop of water, when they were ridden for ten, twelve, or even fourteen hours at a stretch, with merely an hour's rest, without forage at noon. Our escort was an officer mounted on a beautiful Arab."

In " Travels in Three Great Empires, Austria, Russia and Turkey," C. B. Elliott writes :—

" The Bedouins' horses constitute their chief treasure and happiness, and such animals are worthy the partiality they secure. Nothing can exceed the symmetry and grandeur of one of these noble animals. He lies down like a lamb in the midst of the family, gambols with the infant Ishmaelite, and displays a degree of sagacity almost bordering on reason. They travel, as our Sheik informed us, four days and nights without allowing themselves more than an hour each morning for food. After this continuous journey of ninety-six hours, they halt for twenty-four, then resume their progress during another such stage of extraordinary length. In these long intervals no water is to be found, hence the necessity for proceeding without loss of time. In answer to our query how the horses bore this fatigue and deprivation of water, the Sheik replied : ' By the special favour of Allah.'

" Hungarian steeds one learns to appreciate highly for their speed and ease. There are several stud-farms with pure-bred Arabs."

In " Across Persia," E. Crawshay Williams says that all their retinue rode horses which answered perfectly to the popular conception of the " Arab Steed." The Khan's son and another man, armed as if for a campaign, were both mounted on the same horse, which did not seem in the least affected by its double load.

In "Russian, Japanese, and Chunchuse," Ernest Brindle says that the Chunchuse, being splendid horsemen, well-mounted on the best ponies procurable on the hills and plains of Manchuria, make admirable irregulars, and became to the Russian troops formidable enemies; galloping their hardy game little native ponies, at the highest speed, they would swoop down upon the railway.

Colonel J. P. Robertson, author of "Personal Adventures," says that during the Indian Mutiny he took the officers commanding the troops to the horses picketed in the open, 500 well-bred Arabs, thoroughly and perfectly free from vice, which is a characteristic of Arab horses. They soon took to their new masters.

Her late Majesty wrote :—

"As to the horses which I ride, I have got two darlings, both of them quite perfect in every sense of the word : very handsome, full of spirit, delightfully easy-goers, very quiet, and never shying at anything—the one Irish, the other smaller—a dark chestnut with a beautiful little Arabian head" ("Letters of Queen Victoria.").

Mr. Home Davenport, a celebrated breeder, in an article in *Country Life in America*, August, 1906, writes :—

"Our thoroughbreds are tender as hothouse plants, and so nervous and ill-tempered that half of them kill their own chances, thrashing about at the post."

Compared, he says, with the average plater, leggy, weedy, or tucked up in the flank, or crook-legged, or cat-hammed, with but here and there a saving good point, the Arab is compact, yet generous of mould, formed equally for speed and strength, with deep, swelling chest, length everywhere that length counts, and with, above all, power to work all the exquisite mechanism to the very limit of endurance. Then he continues :—

"The Arab is the best and biggest horse of his inches in the world. His heart is in the right place, and is, like

EXCELLENCE OF ARABS

his constitution, so stout that he can not only stay to the end, but come out to race day after day. The weediness, the ill-temper, the lack of conformation in our thoroughbreds mean that the old blood has run out. It needs renewing from the fountain-head: the strain that holds still all the vital vigour of sun and sand. If their blood be liberally infused through the thoroughbreds, we shall see a big percentage of each year's colts credits to the turf and their breeders, instead of, as now, a discredit to both."

In "Twenty Years in Persia," Dr. J. G. Wishard tells us that twenty years ago a splendid riding pony could be bought in Kurdistan for twenty-five dollars, and that the best horses that find their way to the capital come from Arabia and Kurdistan.

G. L. Bell, in "The Desert and the Town," writes:—

"The Anezeh mares are the best in all Arabia, so that even the Shammar seek after them to improve their own breed. In front of us rose the Jebel el 'Ala, apparently a wall of rock, impossible for horses to climb. I rode with an aching heart. It was indescribable. We jumped and tumbled over the rock faces, and our animals jumped and tumbled after us, scrambling along the edge of little precipices, where, if they had fallen, they must have broken every bone. Reshid Agha rode a splendid Arab mare; her every movement was a pleasure to behold."

This is an extract from Church's "Fall of Carthage":—

"Both armies were now on the north bank of the Po. Hannibal's light African troopers, who rode their horses without a bit, were on either wing. The weakness of the Romans in cavalry was fatal. The Carthaginian horse charged on both wings, and routed their opponents almost without a struggle."

"The Crusades," by T. A. Archer and Charles Sethbridge Kingsford, speaks of Baldwin mounted on his fleet Arab. The heavy horses of Richard's cavalry, with their armoured riders, were no match for the swift-footed Arab steeds of the lightly-clad Saracens. It was said that El-Adel, hearing Richard had no horse, sent him two Arab steeds.

In " Things Seen in Morocco," A. J. Dawson writes :—

" The most gallant beast, the bravest, gamest horse ever lapped in hide, Zemouri, munched the last of the Tafilet dates, while Deny crunched up his belt a hole or two, and comforted himself sucking the stones. He grew thin as a rail, and yet pranced all day like a two-year-old, and carried me where no other horse could when he was dying."

Professor Agton, in his " Life of Richard the First," says that Saladin's chief strength consisted in the light Syrian cavalry, largely Arab blood, while the Latins depended upon their foot. The Turkish troops, however, unlike the Christians, with whom disorder was defeat, were easily rallied. They fled only to return to the charge when a fitting opportunity presented itself. Saladin's Arab cavalry was a torment exactly similar to that which a traveller endures when a swarm of hornets circle round his head, buzzing in his ear, and fretting his temper by their continual attempts to sting, for, when almost upon the point of the spears, they whirled round and flung their lances and javelins into the midst of the Crusaders.

We also read that the heavily-armed Germans could not retreat from the activity of the Saracens, who always hovered round them and seized the proper moment and fell upon them with tumultuous rapidity, sword in hand, and men, horses, and baggage were cast into the abyss.

In " The Princes of India," Sullivan says that Shah Jehan, at the head of 100,000 horse, was attended by 100 of the noblest rank mounted on the finest Arabian horses.

Sir Charles Lawson, in his " Memories of Madras," tells us that Colonel Aston " left a favourite Arab horse to Colonel Wellesley." People do not leave screws to their

EXCELLENCE OF ARABS

friends, and I observe generally that writers such as those above cited speak out of the fullness of the heart, and in general are manifestly contrasting the Arab with the English thoroughbred.

Captain Townshend, Military Consul in Turkey, says:—

"The Anatolian horses are mere ponies, 14·2 or 14·3 hands, but they will carry a heavy load for nine or ten hours a day over the worst of mountain paths, and require only about one day's rest in a week. They are lightly built, hardy, wiry, and very surefooted. . . . We came to a broken bridge, with a crack about 2 feet wide in the middle, quite enough to disconcert a heavily-laden English horse, but our country-bred animals thought nothing of it: just jumped across in a clatter of buckets, cooking-pots, tent-poles, and any other odd articles which were tied, Turkish fashion, with bits of string all over the loads. The horses got down as best they could, we watching them as they descended, sometimes making long slides all four feet together. If one of them had lost his balance, he would only have been food for jackals; but they all got somehow to the bottom. No English horse could have done it."

Mr. Spencer Borden, in America, has recently written a book on the Arab horse, of which he has made a speciality after many years' study of the horse in general. He agrees with Professor Ridgeway's opinion of the Arab's excellence, and says that to know the Arab horse is to love him; that from an old book which came into his possession some years ago it would appear that the Arabian horses have always been, and still are, the best in the world; and that their blood has been introduced into common horses from 1,600 to 2,000 years before Christ. He states that no horse but an Arab has ever been found with the courage to face a lion. We have pictures of kings hunting lions on him thousands of years ago. Mr. Borden tells us that Catherine the Great had in the Imperial stud twelve pure Arab stallions and ten Arab mares. I have mentioned the high character given to the Hungarian ponies, and Mr. Borden shows that they have descended from high-caste Arabs taken into the Carpathians by the Turks, and he supplements what Major-General Tweedie said as to the Arab having improved every blood that he has touched, and says that the most intelligent breeders have acknowledged that superior breeding in horses is generally an accumulation of the amount of the Arab blood that they possess.

Although Mr. Borden accepts Professor Ridgeway's statements as to the Arab's excellencies, he does not accept so unreservedly the Professor's view as to the Arabs having no horses in Arabia before Mahomet. He says that for use under saddle, either for pleasure or as cavalry, no horse that ever lived can compare with Arab blood.

A few months ago there appeared, amongst Collins' sixpenny novels, " A Royal Rascal," which I do not quite know how to appreciate. It is from beginning to end an unstinted praise of the Arab horse. All lovers of horses ought to read it. It purports to be the life of an officer in the Peninsula War, but whether all is imagination, or some, and how much ought to be taken as accurate description, each must judge for himself.

A writer in the *National Review* for May, 1910, states that it is not surprising that a horse should possess courage when he traces descent from the Darley Arabian, for courage is a notable characteristic of the Arab.

A German gentleman sent me an *Illustrirte Zeitung* of December 17, 1908, giving a very interesting account of the numerous horse-breeding establishments in Hungary. Even the Church, the writer says, has taken it up. It is altogether too long to quote, but descriptions of several Government studs are given, where there are altogether 10,000 horses under the Minister for Agriculture, of which a great number are full-blood and half-blood Arabs. Numbers were imported from the East. The writer concludes his article by stating that " his full-blood stock gain the highest admiration of the world, and his half-bloods are becoming keen rivals of English horses."

EXCELLENCE OF ARABS

The following extracts are from the *Australasian* of November 26, 1904 :—

"The Arab horse has done good service in crossing with the pony. Mr. A. J. Fisher's handsome and powerful bay Arab, desert-born, is doing good service. For three years in succession his yearlings have carried off the first prize."

On November 28, 1905, Major J. Moore points out that Russian horses have a large infusion of English and Arab blood.

On March 24, 1906, Mr. Wilfred Blunt writes to say that, except where really hard work is being done—hunting or serious journeys—an Arab horse requires no corn at all. He never allows corn to the horses he personally rides.

In "The Adventures of a Civil Engineer," C. O. Burge mentions that in India he kept several horses. The Australian Walers, though hardy enough in their own country, where he met them later, do not stand the Indian climate well. The Arab is the most reliable, and has the most staying-power, and possesses good temper in a marked degree.

The Duke of Argyll records that the Emperor of Austria at his Coronation rode a splendid grey Arab.

In *Harper's Monthly*, March, 1910, Mr. Elsworth Huntington writes that the Arabs often ride 300 or 400 miles to the scene of a raid. They have camels to endure the thirst, but they must have horses to use in the final dash.

Dr. Hume Griffith, a resident in Persia and Turkish Arabia for eight years, tells us that the Arabs are very fond of their horses, and "a true Arab horse is a lovely creature."

In a book published in 1715 on the "Conquest of Syria, Persia, and Egypt by the Saracens," the Rev. S. Ockley gives an account of their customs collected from the most authentic Arabic authors, especially manuscripts.

In the Preface he says that the Arabians were a people as little taken notice of by the Greek and Roman authors as could be well supposed, considering their nearness and the extent of their country. He denounces the Greek writers for their obscurity on the subject, and complains of " the lame accounts " by the Byzantine historians. It is, therefore, no wonder that Professor Ridgeway did not find much in the classics about the Arabs.

But more notable than that is Mr. Ockley's statement that " before Mahomet's time the chief excellency of the Saracens consisted in breeding and managing horses."

One of his most valuable manuscripts was by one Abu Abdollah Mahammed Ebu Omar Alwakidi, "in the invaluable collection of that incomparable prelate and martyr of blessed memory, Archbishop Laud."

He relates, as did my former book, the giving of double spoil to the riders of pure Arab horses after the Battle of Damascus, and adds that the Prophet himself had done so after the Battle of Chaiber.

It is asserted in some quarters that Arab horses cannot jump. Now, that is ridiculous. The celebrated Miss Dillon very recently had a pure Arab mare, not 15 hands, Raschida, which she used in the hunting-field, and won nineteen first prizes in jumping competitions. It carried 13 stone in the hunting field ten weeks before foaling. When trained, they make splendid jumpers. My stallion, Faraoun, jumped a 6-foot post and rail fence three or four days after he arrived from England, and used to love to jump a low fence after his grooming.

CHAPTER VII

EXCELLENCE OF THE ARAB, GATHERED CHIEFLY FROM VARIOUS NEWSPAPERS AND MAGAZINES

IF I cited ancients only, then the modern jockey might pretend that the Arab had died out, and if I cited only recent authorities, then he might say that it was the thoroughbred who had begotten the horses mentioned. If I cited books only, then he might say that the newspaper press of the day could alone be relied upon; and if I cited the newspaper press, then he might say they were writing to please their supporters. So I give him a little of all. But 5,000 years—how much more, no one can say—of almost unanimous praise, down to the present time, prevents these excuses from being raised with advantage.

From the *Times*, October 2, 1908 :—

" At Babolna in Hungary there is an Arab stud claimed to be the largest and most meritorious stud of pure-bred Arab horses outside Arabia, and it is of a very fascinating and interesting character, and the historic breed of Arab is there seen in its original purity, symmetry, and quality. A succession of greys elicited unstinted admiration, and the large group of mares with foals at foot or in foal were wonderfully uniform in size, type, and character. Col. Fadallah, a distinguished Syrian military man, is so enamoured of the qualities of the Eastern horse that he has scant toleration for those of Western origin."

The following extracts, except where otherwise stated, are from the *Australasian* :—

June 2, 1906 :—

" The Welsh pony, Tam O'Shanter, gave one the impression that he had thrown back to some strain of Arab blood in his pedigree."

December 15, 1906 :—

" The best Spanish horses were at one time practically Arabian horses of high breeding. One hundred and fifty years ago the English were importing horses from Arabia and Spain indiscriminately, and both kinds of importations were called Arabians."

On July 28, 1906, Mr. Morrow, a breeder of North Queensland, writes : " The Suffolk Punch crossed with the thoroughbred, then with the pure Arabian, a first, second, or third strain should give us an animal fit for almost every purpose. With a fresh infusion of pure Arabian blood we may hope to produce something of far greater value than we are now doing. Does it not stand to reason that the Arab of Arabia, which has been bred for thousands of years with the utmost care to do a certain kind of work, must be of superlative excellence when called upon, as he is so often in the tribal warfare of the country, to perform journeys taxing his speed and endurance to the utmost ?"

January 5, 1907 :—

" In France, Arabs have been largely used for many years in the Government stud, and their produce, though not as large as the *demi-sang*, give one the idea that they would better withstand the wear and tear of a campaign."

On May 18, 1907, the *Mark Lane Express*, which voices the opinions of most horse-breeders of experience, states that it has always been a puzzle that there should be such a demand for such a size in stallions, since an oversized horse is worse than an undersized one. In any breed the moderate-sized ones are the most successful at the stud, both as sires and as brood mares. The animals that proved their worth in the trying time in the

EXCELLENCE OF THE ARAB

British Army were Arabs and half-bred Arabs, which were little more than ponies. As a rule, the thoroughbred of moderate value is not fit for the purpose : he is too weedy. As a sire for light horses of general utility—such as buggy horses and horses for mounted infantry—there is nothing that can equal the Arab if the right sort can be obtained. They have proved their worth ever since Australia was settled.

Ponies that seem to fulfil all requirements are the Battak ponies from the high mountains of Sumatra. Captain Hayes describes their handsome heads set on high-crested necks, full of spirit and simply balls of muscle. The capable and light-hearted way in which one of these grand Lilliputs can trot away with a four-wheeled vehicle containing five or six heavy men is a sight worth going many miles to see. Battak ponies have almost entirely lost their original type from frequent crossing with imported Arabs.

August 31, 1907 :—

" Sir Rupert Clarke some years ago used Arab stallions at Bolinda Vale, whose stock turned out so well that he wished for another Arab stallion to succeed them."

November 28, 1908 :—

" Mr. C. A. H. Youl is forming a small stud which recalls to mind one of the handsomest Arab mares bred by Mr. James Stewart many years ago, mated with Peter Wilkins ; the result, the handsome Lady Power, a great jumper, and a strain of the blood of some of the early day Arabs brought to this island is worth having in a jumper."

September 14, 1907 :—

" The great Persian traveller, Captain Mark Sykes, states that in Mesopotamia he met Italian officers visiting that country to purchase thoroughbred Arab mares for the Italian breeding stud, and that, like many other Continental Governments, the Italian Government has great faith in the Arab strain to produce horses fit for army purposes. They have courage, staying power, and will stand hard times and hard work that would kill the more showy, upstanding horse which generally realizes much higher prices."

The French Government, official, Charles du Hays, author of the Government Percheron stud book, writes, in the *Country Gentleman*, August 4, 1904, that the Arab was the foundation of Count Orloff's trotters and coach-horses, as well as of the English thoroughbred; and he says that everything we have—good, fine, and distinguished—comes from Arabia, and that he is strictly in favour of breeding in and in.

Major W. S. Maxwell, in the *Badminton*, August, 1904, writes of a little Arab pony in a boar hunt as round on his haunches in a moment—a marvellously quick and handy pony, who, moreover, is just as keen as his rider. He jinks as quick as the pig, and he not only follows him as a greyhound follows a hare through one jink, but two or three more, and the pace is very fast.

The *Mail*, Monday, October 31, 1904, states the men, horses, and camels of Marwar are alike famous for their spirit, endurance, and vitality. Evidently, these must be Arab.

From the *South African Register*, January, 1905 :—

" Mr. Harmiston has been breeding horses from Arab sires. He has some fine young stock, and he had not the least difficulty in putting the bridle on a young filly running in a good-sized paddock. He rode her barebacked, got on and off on the offside, sat on her quarters, and then slid off behind, the filly standing quite still all the time."

The *Badminton*, January, 1905 :—

" Lippieza was founded in 1580 by the Archduke Carl, and its original breed was from the Spanish horse of the Pyrenees, which the long Moorish domination had strongly crossed with Arab and Berber blood. They have a strong constitution, and develop tardily, frequently

EXCELLENCE OF THE ARAB

retaining their full strength until thirty years old. Three different breeds are kept in Lippieza: (1) Descendants of the old Lippieza race; (2) descendants of pure-blood Oriental race, for which stallions were imported from the desert; (3) a crossing between Lippieza and the pure Arab. The mortality is extremely small."

The *Farmer and Grazier* of January 20, 1905, gives an American's opinion that, although the Arab horse is only a pony, yet as regards his general make-up and substance, vigour, resolution, strength, and staying powers, courage, boldness, sobriety, the soundest legs and feet, and his extraordinary lung power, extraordinary eyesight, good temper, tractability, instinct, and sagacity, and for his size he is a wonderful weight carrier. Further, it is not uncommon for a pure Arab horse to cover from 125 to 150 miles in twenty-four hours, and this without food or water until his journey is finished.

A writer in the *Badminton Magazine*, February, 1905, says that he was shown the white Arab which King Humbert used to ride, with beautiful eyes like all good Arab horses, and a condescending manner. The Texan pony is far better suited to polo than the thoroughbred. He is a direct descendant of the Spanish Barbs taken to Mexico. Over a long distance he would be found loping comfortably along with never a hair turned, when the thoroughbred were dead from exhaustion. In turning he is quicker than any horse on earth. Neither does he lack intelligence. He will remain as cool-headed and keep as close an eye on the ball at polo, and take as keen an interest in the game, as the most veteran player. The saddle ponies thus far produced in America are the result of crossing imported Arabs on various breeds of native stock, trotting-bred, plains-bred, or Morgan.

The *Advertiser* in 1905 quoted the *Sydney Daily Telegraph* as saying the horse of to-day has deteriorated, and giving many instances of staying powers of Arab stock, and affirming that they are by far the best breed of horse.

Scribner's, August, 1905 :—

" The horses of Turkestan are the descendants of those which carried Tamerlane and his victorious army from Samarkand to the Nile, and almost to Constantinople, and from Asia Minor to the gates of Moscow and back again to Samarkand. They are large, strong, and fat, and full of endurance, showing many traces of Arabian blood. The Turkoman is a born horseman and born judge of horseflesh. These Turkestan horses have through the ages been improved again and again by Arab stallions."

From *Good Words*, 1905 :—

" During the first three centuries of our era the prosperity of North Africa was great. Even in those days the Arab horse was renowned and of considerable value. The speed of travelling then was surprisingly rapid. Tiberius is said to have hastened to his dying brother, covering 200 miles in twenty-four hours."

In an article in the *Fortnightly Review* a writer mentions that the horses were the heroes of the journey, although not the Arab steed of poetry, a lover of which would be disappointed by the Syrian creature; but after a while, when he saw it pick its way amid endless perils and stones, with never a slip or stumble which it could not recover from, he would grow to think that steadiness is a finer quality than dash. The Syrian Arab is three-fourths pure Arab.

According to the *Express* of October 23, 1905, Marvel Loch, who won the Caulfield Cup that year, had a recent Arab sire in her pedigree, Satellite.

The *Illustrated Sporting and Dramatic News* in December, 1905, stated that Lieutenant-Colonel Heath rode and drove his forty-five years old horse, Nugget, foaled November, 1869, dam an Arab mare, several times from Melbourne to Shepparton in two days. When mustering cattle, a 100 miles a day did not seem to distress him.

From *Blackwood's Magazine*, February, 1906 :—

" The Mexicans said that many of their ponies were capable of carrying a heavy man, with his two-stone

EXCELLENCE OF THE ARAB

weight of paraphernalia, fifty miles a day for a whole fortnight, with no grooming and only such forage as they could pick up round their halting at night. These ponies are greatly built up with Arab blood introduced into America by the Spaniards."

The *Argus*, March 1, 1906 :—

" Mr. F. Austin, Mr. P. Kellady, Mr. J. L. Wheeler, and Mr. D. Wind all favour a mixture of Arab blood." On the 5th of the same month it observes that Mr. James Rankin, Mr. G. Maddison, and Mr. J. K. Morrison are of the same opinion, and on the 9th it quotes H. W. Farrall as saying that no horse approaches the Arab as a sire to produce the horses under discussion.

Mr. Joseph Carwardine, dealer in stock, writes that amongst his brother's stud of blood mares in Northern Australia were several half-bred Arabs, and the residents of that district agreed that anything with Arab blood in them had better legs and would stand work better than any other breed.

The *Cultivator and Country Gentleman*, June 14, 1906 :—

" The pure Arabian horse is the only thoroughbred horse on earth ; the soundest, most healthy, the most enduring, the most intelligent, the most easily taught, and possessed of a memory that would be wonderful even in a human being." The writer bred Naomi to Anejah, a pure-bred Seglawi Jedram Arab. The result was a model of perfection, mental and physical.

The *Ladies' Field*, June 29, 1906 :—

" The Arab type comes out with startling clearness in the ponies of the New Forest. The Arab has a constitution patient of hardship, and there is enough Arab blood running in the veins of the New Forest pony to make him a better saddle pony than almost any other breed."

The *Windsor Magazine*, November, 1905 :—

" Great travellers have declared that no praise, however generous, does proper justice to the Arab horse.

Those who have travelled in the East have enjoyed his easy pace, his sure foot, and his tireless activity; have responded with pleasure to his affectionate disposition and ready recognition of gentle treatment; while the modern thoroughbred has lost his original good qualities and is deteriorating steadily."

Life, November 15, 1906 :—

" The Arab is compact, formed equally for speed and strength, with deep swelling chest, length everywhere; but length counts in shoulders, quarters, arms, with, above all, the impression of power to work all this exquisite mechanism to the very limit of endurance. He has gentleness of disposition and sweetness of temper, and is the best and biggest horse of his inches in the world. His heart is in the right place, and is like his constitution, so stout that he not only stays to the end, but comes out to race day after day."

The Mizza had high-bred Arab mares, and in the evening would sit in the inner court amongst them.

On one occasion, Layard accompanied a Government messenger who provided him with one horse, and they galloped day and night until they reached Mosul, in little more than fifty hours, a distance of about 250 miles. The Arabs in those districts did not use bridles, but managed their horses with halters.

The powers of the Arab are most wonderful. His excellence is in his blood and powers of continuance under fatigue, and the true breed may be considered the most perfect model in the equine race. Richard Lawrence, a highly-educated man, who gave his entire life to the study of the horse, every time came back to the Arabian horse, smaller in size than the cart horse, but far more powerful in proportion to his size.

In the *Bulletin* of January 1, 1907, a writer tells how in the early nineties, seeking medical aid for his wife, he rode an Arab more than 220 miles in seventy-two hours through heavy black soil in drenching rain.

EXCELLENCE OF THE ARAB

Elder's Weekly Review :—

"A Kirghiz chief galloped with a Cossack escort (with two horses per man) 200 miles in twenty-four hours, a considerable part of the distance being mountainous and rocky. The horses were a little lame for the first few days, but soon recovered."

Blackwood's Magazine, February, 1907 :—

"After three or four bottles of claret the Nabob would, in the middle of the night, order out his horse and ride like a madman along the cliffs always at top speed. If the horse he rode—an Arab he had brought from the East—had not been more like a goat than a horse, he must have broken his neck in some of these fearsome gallops."

The *Producers' Review*, February 6, 1907 :

"The hardiest horse in the world is the Arab, and he ought not to be above 14 hands or at the most 14·2 hands."

Ladies' Field, April 12, 1907 :—

"The American trotter sire is, of course, a horse of mixed origin, and, even if the first cross is successful, there is always a chance that the second generation may be a failure, so that his foals should be crossed with an Arab. The success of the Continental breeders in producing useful troop horses is greatly due to their use of half-bred Arab mares."

The Barb which escaped from the Spaniards in South America quickly established breeds of undoubted merit. The Arabian horse's bone is denser and stronger than that of any other breed, whilst his muscles are strengthened enormously by elastic tissue which is interwoven among the muscles. Since it is this which gives him great endurance and strength, Arabian blood has been a great improvement to every breed in the world.

The *Montreal Herald* in 1907 feared that the ancient breed of Arabian horses to which the British thoroughbred, the American trotting horses, and the Orloff trotters owe their best qualities, was in danger of becoming extinct, but trusts that this fear no longer exists. The last ten years has largely increased the number of persons who are disposed to breed the Arab and recognize his wonderful qualities.

Mr. Hernan Hoopes, the celebrated American breeder, writes that at their Stallion Shows about a hundred stallions paraded the town behind a brass band, and his Arab was always put next to the band because the thoroughbreds and trotters would not stand the band. They yelled and fussed so greatly that their grooms could not hold them, whereas the Arab did not mind it any more than if they had made no sound.

Chambers' Journal, October 16, 1907 :—

"General Havelock was as erect on his chestnut Arab as if his threescore and two years meant nothing, in a storm of round and grape shot, variegated with musketry, filling the air with hurtling, hissing noises.

The *Pastoralists' Review*, November 15, 1907 :—

"Mr. Blunt crossed Arabs with Suffolks in order to get carriage horses of a fair size, which would do long-journey work of thirty or forty miles a day during his annual driving tours, with the result that he obtained the precise animal he wanted, so excellent and so untirable that after six seasons driving them he came to the conclusion that they will probably last him the remainder of his days. The Arab-Suffolks are from 15·2 to 15·3 hands, with admirable legs and feet. They can trot from eight to ten miles an hour and keep it up."

Harper's Magazine, January, 1908 :—

"There is something very attractive about these Arabian horses. They are spirited, fearless, surefooted, and yet as a rule so docile that they may be ridden with a halter, and are good for a long journey or a swift run. An Arabian stallion satisfies the romantic ideal of how a horse ought to look : arched neck, small head, large eyes, short body, round flanks, delicate pasterns, and little feet. When you see the swiftness and spring of his gallop, the dainty grace of his walk, you recognize the real original horse which the painters used to depict in their portraits."

The *National Review*, April, 1908 :—

" In the French operations in Morocco the Spahis provided their own horses and they mounted themselves on very good barbs, which kept their condition well, and could move fast when wanted to."

The *Badminton Magazine*, May, 1908 :—

" The barb horses are grand riding animals. The authoress was once called upon to give up an expedition or take a flying leap over a chasm 5 or 6 feet wide and 30 or 40 feet deep, and her horse made light work of it."

Munsey's Magazine, May, 1908 :—

" The gem and pet of the royal stables of the Kaiser is the little red sorrel Arabian mare, called Irene, purchased at a great price by the Kaiser as a gift to his only daughter. This beautiful little creature is the ideal of a lady's horse and has been highly educated. She was taken on Christmas Eve up the steps and into the large hall of the New Palace to be presented to her future owner."

The *National Review*, June, 1908 :—

" The writer objected that at Klangwane ponies could not climb between these stones, and they had better walk ; but he was told it would be a foolish thing to trust to his own legs instead of the ponies, who showed that they knew how to place their feet a sight better than any human being, and with their reins hanging loose on their necks they plodded up."

Cornhill Magazine, June, 1908 :—

" All through the centuries the Arab helped on the ancient breed by careful mating, always retaining the finest mares to carry on the priceless strain. Arab blood was brought to England earlier than the Norman Conquest, and more than likely that the Romans brought Eastern blood as well. Later, King John, Edward III., and Henry VIII. were all importers of Eastern blood. Thus, the English horse had no inconsiderable dash of Arab in him when the Godolphin Arabian, the Byerly Turk, the Darley Arabian, and the Royal mares of Charles II. found their way to these islands."

The *Queenslander*, October 19, 1908, quotes Lord Roberts writing of his Arab horse, Maidan: " I bought him in Bombay in 1877. He was a pure-bred Nejd Arab. The following year I took him to Afghanistan, where he was with me in extreme heat, cold, and very often with difficulties about proper food for him. But while other horses fell off in condition from not getting forage, he maintained his throughout. I kept him all the time I was in India, and in 1893 brought him to England. He attracted great attention at the late Queen's Jubilee in 1897. During the twenty-two years he was in my possession he travelled with me 50,000 miles and was never sick or sorry. He measured exactly 14·2 hands."

Maidan was with Lord Roberts during the great march from Cabul to Kandahar, and twelve years previously he had carried Lieutenant-Colonel Brownlow, of the 72nd Highlanders, who weighed 210 pounds. He was then shipped to England from Bombay, and stood on his feet without lying down during 100 days on the passage to Marseilles, and was unblemished at twenty-three, when he had to be destroyed because of a broken leg.

In the *Garden and Field*, South Australia, Mr. I. Selth, a very experienced horseman, advises breeders that they should introduce more Arabian blood, as our horses are degenerating from what they were forty years ago. Speaking from personal knowledge of two mares, one half-bred, the other with a good strain of Arab blood, he says it mattered not how long the journey or how scant the food, it was next to impossible to knock either of them up. The latter carried a man 12 stone from Kadina to Adelaide, a distance of 100 miles, in less than twelve hours, while he himself rode her fifty miles on an urgent message in five hours, and the mare did not seem the least distressed. A friend of Mr. Selth's, of great experience, once wrote: " The Arab for saddle and light harness work on a farm is invaluable. He is intelligent, docile, quick, and graceful in his movements, and useful in every way. He excels all other breeds it has been my fortune to possess."

Mr. W. P. Auld, one of Stuart's celebrated band of explorers who were the first to cross the Australian continent, states that in their party was a little Arab to which they used to trust for any extra hard travelling, for there was no knocking him up. They used to pile on him bits of loads from the others when they were tired, and he used to go down on his knees to have his loading taken off.

In the Emperor Frederick's diary it is stated they had to ride over smooth slopes of rock and interminable loose, rolling stones, and he feared every minute that his little Barbary steed would loose his footing. But these clever, tough little animals know no difficulties and never even stumble.

The *Sydney Stock and Station Journal*, April 23, 1909:—

"On the birth of an Arab colt of noble breed it is usual to assemble some witnesses and write an account of the colt's distinctive marks, with the names of its sire and dam. The mares will average at least six times as much as the horses, and the Arabs seldom consent to sell the whole of a mare. The Arabs ascribe the good qualities of the colt rather to the dam than to the sire."

Blackwood's Magazine, September, 1909:—

" The Sikh cavalry is as good as most, and they generally beat us at polo. In 1907, the Patiala team carried off the Beresford Cup from the 17th Lancers; and the Patiala Imperial service troops, after a review by Lord Kitchener, performed a manœuvre in which two squadrons of Lancers galloped up, dismounted, and threw their horses on the ground, where they lay still, while another squadron came galloping up behind and subsided in the same mysterious manner 50 yards ahead."

The *Express*, November 20, 1909 :—

"A party, among which were Mr. Bury and Mr. Gething, last summer tried to penetrate into South Arabia, anxious to reach the buried cities in the interior. They got away from Irka with an escort of fifteen men and eight camels, but the caravan was stopped. The Chief Haura would not send them food, and he set a guard over them. Every now and again the Arabs fired pot shots at them for amusement ! After five anxious days, the Chief Haura sent them a final letter ordering them to leave his country within three hours. Having lived mainly on jam and biscuits, the prospect of a flight of thirty-five miles was not a pleasant one. They had to discard their baggage, for their escort deserted. The following morning, the Chief said he would send camels and demanded all their money, which was handed over, and in the evening twenty-seven camels arrived. Shots were fired at them at intervals. They started on their return journey to the coast, which they at last reached absolutely done up."

CHAPTER VIII

ARAB HORSES AS PRESENTS

IT may be of some interest if I here set forth an account of a few presents of Arab horses, made to various kings and nobles at different times, which have happened to be recorded in history, and which may have been given as part of the terms for purchasing peace after a war.

None would contend that any present of anything ordinary made by one person to another in an ordinary way was in every case evidence of its excellence; but, when we find through all history that presents of Arab horses have been deemed proper presents to offer to a king, and worthy of acceptance by many of the greatest rulers of the world, it must be taken as proof of more than ordinary excellence. Besides, givers in the old time would be very careful not to offend a king, who might cut off the giver's head at a moment's notice if he offered trash. What made the present of an Arab horse so general was not merely the knowledge of his excellence, but the knowledge that the pure Arab was rare, and the knowledge that it was exceedingly difficult and generally impossible to procure a mare. The extreme care which the Arabs took as to their breeding and as to guarding and preserving their mares was universally recognized, and those of undoubted pure breed were even in Nejd known to be comparatively few; indeed, I doubt if

1 per cent. of the horses called Arabs have ever been of the pure breed, and even in Nejd I should doubt if 20 per cent. were so. Hence their value, and the efforts of all peoples riding horses to procure pure Arabs, and the reasonable certainty that a great and warlike king would be sure to do his utmost to try and secure one. The foal of an Arab mare foaled in Nejd would almost certainly be pure, but that could not be always affirmed with certainty of a foal born anywhere else, even from a pure mare. Xenophon tells us that, at a great feast during the retreat of the 10,000, Seuthes, a Thracian chief, was offered a white horse, and at the same time a horn full of wine was drunk to him, with the words, " I drink to you, O Seuthes, and present you with this horse, on which you will pursue your enemies."

Mr. E. H. Parker, in "A Thousand Years of the Tartars," says that Meghder Khan (100 B.C.), one of the greatest conquerors of the world's history, sent a present of Tartar horses to the Empress of China, and the Turkish Khan sent a present of horses to the founders of the T'ang Dynasty, and a number of Persian mares were obtained by the Turks. Their offspring acquired great repute for swiftness about A.D. 1200.

In the *Woman at Home*, January, 1905, Constance Beerbohm writes that " a splendid Arab, Ruheil by name, had been presented by the Sultan of Turkey to the Crown Prince."

The *Advertiser*, February 21, 1905 :—

" After the taking of Port Arthur, General Stoessel begged General Nogi to accept his beautiful Arab charger as a present, and General Nogi accepted it on behalf of the Japanese Army."

The Anglo-Saxon Kings were bitten with the craze for racing, whether they derived it from the Roman Conquest or not. In the reign of Athelstan, the father of

ARAB HORSES AS PRESENTS

Hugh Capet could find no gift more appropriate than some "running horses." Alexander, King of Scotland, presented one to a church in A.D. 1121, and his companion, which was a gift from Eastern Europe, was kept in the Royal stud at Gillingham. At Hastings, William the Conqueror rode a small Eastern stallion of 14 hands, given him by Alfonso of Spain. Favell and Lyard, the favourite steeds of Richard Cœur-de-Lion, were valued at £1,000. John imported some from the East, and the gifts of barb stallions to Roger de Belesme, Earl of Shrewsbury, also enriched the Royal stud.

Black Saladin was slain by his master at the Battle of Barnet in April, 1476, to encourage his followers to fight better on foot, and his gravestone may still be seen in the ground of Warwick Hotel on the eastern Barnet Road.

It was announced by the *Daily Telegraph* (London) that the late King Edward presented the Sultan with a thoroughbred horse. This suggests a most interesting reversal of an order of things which has lasted for very many centuries, and has probably done more to improve the breed of horses than any other royal custom. The royal mares by their very name recall the ancient precedent by which the monarchs of the East exchange their courtesies with cousins of the Western thrones. But these were almost always stallions; mares were very rarely given away. No Arab parted with his mare, however unfortunate his circumstances, if it could possibly be avoided. High-bred stallions, however, were the favourite gifts of Eastern Princes, and of the three Arab sires to whom English racing stock can now be traced one at least had just such a royal origin.

The pure Arab type is so persistent, and has always been the type of the pure Arabian, that the points for which he is famous at the present day are almost precisely those which led Mahomet to lay the foundations of his famous cavalry in the breed of Nejd. Such was the Arab of Mahomet's warriors, and such you may see him in Mr. Wilfred Blunt's paddocks at the present day. The Emperor Severus, it is said, brought to Wetherby the first Arabs that ever trod Yorkshire. That shows what this Emperor thought of Arabs; but I believe that Arabs had trodden Yorkshire long before.

In April, 1532, one Powle received 7s. 2d. for making a bath for one of the Arabian racers then at Windsor. In March, 1532, "the boy that ran" the Barbary horse received a reward of 18s. 4d. In the spring, 1514, Giovanni Ratti took a present of four thoroughbred horses from the Marquis Mantua to Henry VIII. Henry's letter of thanks to the Marquis is extant, thanking him most heartily for those "most beautiful high-bred and unsurpassed horses just sent to us." These we hold highly welcome and acceptable." The King also had a stallion of Eastern blood given to him by the Duke of Urbino. In 1515, Ferdinand of Arragon, King of Spain, sent to Henry two excellent horses.

Sir Thomas Edmonds brought to England, to the royal paddocks of Newmarket, Barbary horses in November, 1617. The Earl of Salisbury presented the King of Denmark with one of his Barbary horses in 1614. In 1623 Buckingham imported a cargo of the best horses obtainable. It was written of an Arab horse of about that time: "So did his horse excel a common one in shape, in courage, colour, pace, and bone. What a horse should have he did not lack, save a proud rider on so proud a back."

In 1539, the Emperor Charles V. of Spain sent twenty-five beautiful Spanish horses to Henry VIII. He also sent to Edward VI. a present of two most beautiful Spanish horses which were received in London on March 26, 1550 (mentioned by Bishop Hooper in his letter to Henry Bullinger). Mr. Hore quotes Jervis Markham in his quaint work on "How to chuse, ride, and train, and diet Hunting and Running Horses," printed in 1599, as recommending the courser of Arabia as the beau-ideal stallion to breed from for the turf, and as being of reasonable stature, neither too high nor too low—peerless—"for he hath in him the purity and virtue of all other horses." The Queen had a racing establishment for her Barbary horses, which was well replenished with those noble animals.

In "Tunis: Land and People," the Chevalier de Hesse Waitegg wrote that "only two years ago the Pasha Bey presented the King of Spain with a magnificent Arabian horse, and he describes the Bedouins as mounted on beautiful long-tailed horses."

The Bedouin Prince Ibn Rishid made a yearly gift of a mare to the great Syrian Pasha, Mohammed Said.

"Alexander I., King of Scotland, presented to the Church of St. Andrews an Arabian horse."

The *Century Magazine*, November, 1904, states that ancient Chinese records show that about 100 B.C. the Emperor sent to Turkestan for horses which had been improved by breeding, which, as we repeatedly read, was of course by Arab blood.

In "Horses Past and Present," Sir Walter Gilbey, Bart., tells us that the "Privy Purse Expenses" refer to "the Barbaranto horse" and "the Barbary horse" sent by the Marquis of Mantua. Oliver Cromwell imported many Arab Barbs. Charles II. sent his Master of Horse abroad to purchase stallions and brood mares, principally Arabs, Barbs, and Turkish horses. "During the first seventy years of the eighteenth century Eastern horses were imported in large numbers. There is in existence a list of 200 stallions which were sent to this country, but that number does not represent a tithe of the whole."

In "The History of Newmarket," J. P. Hore relates that the Archbishop of Canterbury wrote in November, 1637, that an ambassador had just arrived from the Emperor of Morocco with four valuable Barbary horses for the King.

He also relates that Cardinal Mazarin presented Colonel Lockhart, Cromwell's Ambassador at the Court of France, with four exceedingly fine Arab horses, which Lockhart pronounced to be the finest he ever saw.

"The Chronicle of the Cid," from the Spanish, tells us that the Cid sent a present to King Alfonso of 200 horses, saddled and bridled.

"The History of the Tartars, Moguls, and other Nomadic Tribes of Asia," has frequent accounts of presents of horses made by Kings and Princes to other Kings and Princes.

Professor Freeman mentions that after the defeat of the Saracens in the Taurus in the seventh century, the Commander of the Faithful once more purchased peace by an annual tribute of 3,000 pieces of gold, 50 slaves, and 50 Arab horses.

Layard tells us that the Ruteu-nu took tribute to the Egyptians in the time of Thotines III., amongst which brood mares are particularly mentioned; and quotes 2 Kings xviii. 23 as showing that horses were offered by the Jews to the Assyrian King as an acceptable present. They are mentioned as a suitable tribute by the people of Mesopotamia to the Egyptians. Layard, towards the conclusion of his argument on this, says, "It may, therefore, be conjectured that they were of the most noble, celebrated breeds." Most certainly none but the very best would be offered to a king.

CHAPTER IX

ARAB HORSES IN ENGLAND IN EARLY TIMES

ARAB horses have been for many centuries in England. The Romans undoubtedly brought them over. Some authorities believe that they were in England long before the Romans, and even more surely in Ireland.

The *Nineteenth Century*, June, 1894, informs us that King John and Edward III. purchased Spanish chargers, and that the Crusades showed the excellence of the horses of the Saracens, some of which found their way to England, and led to the development of greater quality in the English light-bred horses, and to the improvement of the heavier type.

Fry's Magazine for June, 1910, notices the disappearance of matches, it having become a complicated business. The first match the writer told of was in 1661, when George Rutherfurdi's Barb ran, which shows that more than 250 years ago the Barb breed of horses were used for racing purposes in Scotland.

The *Gentleman's Magazine* for October, 1905, states that " The Earl has rescued from oblivion the picturesque Eastern pedigree of an Arab horse, Dervish, presented to the King in 1773."

The *Country Gentleman* recently mentioned that from 1780 to 1840 the " English blood horse," known to-day as the English thoroughbred, was almost entirely of Arab and Barb blood.

In the " History of Newmarket and Annals of the Turf," vol. ii., we are told that the Spanish match resulted in the importation to England of some of the best strains of Eastern blood possible to be obtained ; also that Sir Thomas Bendish, the English Ambassador at Constantinople, in September, 1657, procured some Arabian horses for Cromwell.

In " A Varied Life," General E. T. Gordon tells us that the British horse received its first cross in the time of Cassibellamus, and became a compound of those from every province from which the Roman cavalry was supplied ; and that an old metrical romance records the excellence of Richard Cœur-de-Lion's horses purchased at Cyprus, therefore, probably of Eastern origin.

Mr. W. C. L. Martin, in his " History of the Horse," says that in our islands the relics of a large species, equalling a cart-horse in stature, are found ; and that, whenever fine, well-made horses are seen, they are the result of repeated crossings with the best breeds of Arabia or Persia. He adds that the intertropical regions of India are so unfavourable to the horse that the chiefs of Rajpootanah were supplied by Persian merchants with horses of a superior quality : a mixture of Turkoman, Bokhara, and Arab.

Mr. Thomas F. Dale, in Sir Humphrey de Trafford's book, writes that all thoroughbred horses trace back their origin to Eastern ancestors, and that indeed all the light horses of the world owe much to Arab blood. The racehorse, hunters, hackneys, carriage horses, and even our native ponies, he considers, boast some Arab blood.

In " England's Horses for Peace and War," Mr. Vere de Vere Hunt says, on the authority of Youatt, that the Barb was very early introduced into Great Britain to improve the horse.

In " The Horse in History," Basil Tozer tells us that the Earl of Shrewsbury imported from Spain a number of stallions of great value, which greatly improved the breed of horses in Britain, and from the time of the Conquest onward the improvement was distinctly noticeable. King John imported a number of Arab stallions, and Wolsey's Eastern sires are said to have been among the most valuable breeding stock ever known. Henry VIII. imported the best stallions and some of the best mares procurable from Italy, Spain, Turkey, and elsewhere. In Elizabeth's reign a number of Barbs, also many Spanish horses descended from Barbs, were obtained from captured foreign vessels. In Shakespeare's time, the Barbary horse was highly esteemed. Blunderville mentions that fully a century before the Byerly Turk was brought over he himself had seen horses come from Turkey into England, "indifferentlie faire to the eie tho' not verie great nor stronghe, made yet very light and swift in the running, and of great courage." About 1617, half a dozen Barbary horses were brought to England by Sir Thomas Edmunds, and the majority of the best of English mares were crossed with Arabian stallions, and a succession of such stallions was imported throughout the early and the Middle Ages. At the beginning of the era of the Saxon Kings, an Arab steed had come to be looked upon as a recognized royal gift. My readers will notice that in many other countries it was the same.

An inscription in the Castle of St. Angelo at Rome gives the names of forty-two winners of chariot races in the second half of the first century, of which thirty-seven were Libyan, *i.e.*, Barb or Arab.

CHAPTER X

MR. WILFRID BLUNT AND PROFESSOR RIDGEWAY

MR. WILFRID BLUNT has done more to get the Arab horse known than any other half-dozen men living, and is as well known in connection with the Arab as Alexander the Great was with regard to Bucephalus; and Lady Anne Blunt, his wife, has written some exceedingly interesting books on their travels in Arabia, or the Arab horse, which I recommend all interested to read. I shall not quote Mr. Blunt at any length, except in respect of a difference between him and Professor Ridgeway which appears in some observations of Mr. Blunt's in an article in the *Nineteenth Century Magazine*, concerning a book recently written by this celebrated Professor (Professor of Archæology in Cambridge) on the origin of the thoroughbred horse.

This book of Professor Ridgeway's decidedly demonstrates the purity of the Arab horse and his wonderful excellence and superiority. I use the word " purity " in its ordinary sense, viz., of a breed which has been bred pure for a very long period, in this case, I believe, for at least four or five millenniums, for I suppose that nothing exists in this world that is absolutely pure, not even Scotch whisky. I adopt all that the Professor says concerning the Arab's excellence. Indeed, many of his authorities are quoted in my former book—before his was published, I think—and it is satisfactory to me to be so supported by such a great authority.

MR. BLUNT AND PROFESSOR RIDGEWAY

Professor Ridgeway gives us an account of the antideluvian predecessors of the present horse deduced from the fossils—Oro-hippus, Proto-hippus, Hipparion, neo-Hipparion, and other long-named ancestors, *et id genus omne*.

So far as regards Hipparion and these other creatures, and the evidence derived from geology, I yield at once to Professor Ridgeway, and I would not presume to differ from him. But, however interesting and however desirable it is for us to know all about these curious animals of the distant past, such learning has nothing to do with the practical part of the subject.

No farmer need study, no racing man need bother himself to read up, the history and development of those antediluvian animals. A racing man would rather know that his sprinter could do his mile in record time than learn that his sprinter's ancient ancestor in the beginning of the world had five toes; and the farmer would prefer to find that his roadster could draw two tons than that his ancient ancestor had a different-shaped tail from that of the present horses. My readers can learn from the Professor's book all about these things if they want to look it up, and most interesting it is.

As Professor Ridgeway is a man of high authority, I shall quote a few of his statements, taken quite at random, which prove the supreme excellence of the Arab, and which of themselves more than justify my former encomiums on that noble creature, for in proving the excellence of the thoroughbred the Professor proves still more the excellence of the Arab, since without the Arab there could have been, and would be, no thoroughbreds. All the good which is in the thoroughbred is derived from the Arab. It is the wonderful prepotency of the Arab blood which actually keeps the thoroughbred going as a race-horse. Those of the Professor's statements that I refer to in themselves negative to a certain extent his contention that the Arabs had no horses before the time of Christ.

He gives numerous specific instances of the improvement of a nation's breed of horses by Arab stallions, and then he says that from at least 1,000 B.C. there has been a constant demand in Asia for Arab horses.

He says that extraordinary docility characterized the Libyan horse and its derivative, the Arab, and he gives instances. He remarks that the horses of Southern Spain, derived directly from Libya, were noted for the same docility, and their descendants, the Pampas horses of South America, retain that quality, not one word of which can, I think, be disputed, except that I would say " the Arab horse and its derivative, the Libyan," instead of " the Libyan horse and its derivative, the Arab." Mr. Wilfrid Blunt would, I believe, say the same.

A notable example of the superiority of Arab blood is to be found in the Landes horses, which were partly Arab; and, when crossed with the English thoroughbred, the results have always been bad, but when mated with the Arab the results are excellent.

The Suffolk Punch was improved by Arab blood.

The best " English " horses known on the Continent in the fifteenth century were the Irish horses, and they and the swiftest horses in Homeric days, as also in Rome, were owing really to the Arab.

These and other quotations show that Professor Ridgeway's book is full from beginning to end of allusions proving the superiority of the Arab, which seem to me to have the more value as being written, not so much in order to prove the excellence of the Arab horse, as links in the chain of proof with regard to the origin of the thoroughbred horse, and which, therefore, tell much more in favour of the Arab than if the Professor had written

MR. BLUNT AND PROFESSOR RIDGEWAY

for the express purpose of proving the Arab's excellence, as I confess that I do. It is worthy of note, too, that the Professor himself frequently uses the word " Arab " when writing of this horse, although he thinks he came from Libya. He is, indeed, from his high literary status, a more powerful advocate of the Arab blood than I.

He writes that the horse, although indigenous in Upper Asia, was not a native of Arabia, and that the testimony of Erastothenes and Strabo puts it beyond all doubt that the Arabs did not breed or even possess horses until after the beginning of the Christian era. But, in " A Popular Handbook of Bayblonian Archæology," F. C. Norton states that the horse ran wild, and was common in Chaldæa and was often hunted. It was also, he says, domesticated there, and, as Chaldæa borders on Arabia, it seems to me impossible to think that the Arabs would not possess so useful and necessary an animal, frisking about, so to speak, under their very noses.

It is a gratification to me to know that Mr. Blunt differs from the Professor's view that there were no horses in Arabia prior to the time of Christ, and that the Arabs did not even then possess horses, but that it is the Libyan —the modern Barb—which is the fountain of all thorough breeding. Mr. Wilfrid Blunt supports the view which I adopted in my earlier book, and has fallen rather sharply on the Professor for what he thinks his erroneous views on this part of the question in an article in the *Nineteenth Century Magazine* for January, 1906, which is well worth reading.

As to the history of the horse since man first used him, I hold that any ordinary English gentleman is as capable as the Professor of forming an opinion as to the time in which the Arabians became possessed of horses, and I think that Mr. Blunt, by reason of his thorough acquaintance with Arabia, is more likely than Professor Ridgeway to have formed a correct judgment on that point.

Mr. Blunt's fame as an Arabian traveller is world-wide. He has lived with his wife in Arabia amongst the Bedouins for various periods for many years, and no other European knows as much about the Arabs and Arab horses in Arabia as Mr. Blunt does. In the *Nineteenth Century Magazine*, August, 1904, Mr. John M. Bacon affirms that no more experienced or adventurous explorer ever penetrated into the Arabian interior than Mr. Blunt.

I must, however, remind my readers that, although there is a great difference between the two gentlemen regarding the time of appearance of the Arab horse in Arabia, and as to the real country of his origin, there seems no difference at all between them as to his long and honourable history and as to his actual excellence and his wonderful superiority. Both agree that he is unequalled, and all Professor Ridgeway's facts and reasoning go to prove it. It rather seems to me that the real dispute is about a word, a name, not as to what the horse is, but as to whether he comes first from Barbary or earlier from Arabia—a point which I do not propose to discuss, as being wholly unnecessary from my point of view.

The horse about which I am writing is the same horse written of by Professor Ridgeway, known everywhere as the Arab, which the Professor describes as the origin of the thoroughbred, the horse which at various times and places has been spoken of for ages as Arab, although occasionally called Eastern, Asiatic, Turk, Oriental, Barb, and Libyan, but which has always been celebrated, and which the Professor himself at times calls Arab. This difference of nomenclature was natural, and, indeed, almost inevitable, but whatever word was used, the same horse now called Arab was meant. Who ever hears now of a Libyan horse, even in Libya? He is either Arab or Barb.

An Englishman of the seventeenth century, buying him in Morocco, would call him a Barb or Arab indifferently. A Roman of the time of Hannibal would call him Libyan. An Englishman of the fifteenth century, buying him in Turkey, would call him a Turk, or, buying him in Syria, would call him an Eastern horse, and so on. Many of these bought in this way were not pure. They were termed by the Arabs " sons of horses," not " sons of mares," which means not pure on both sides. The only place where he was reliably pure was Arabia, where he was bred in Nejd, whence the Arabs would not sell their mares, and whither the enemy could not come to steal them.

I must point out that several of the authorities which I shall quote speak of horses as Arabs which are notoriously only partly and not pure Arabs. Many Syrian horses are called Arabs which the Bedouins, the real breeders of the pure Arab, deny to be Arab, and call " sons of horses." They deny that they are " sons of mares," *i.e.*, of Arab mares. The sires of " sons of horses " may be pure, but their dams are not; the dams may be of any breed. They are generally admirable horses by reason of the share of Arab blood which they do possess, but nevertheless are not pure-bred Arab horses. But the wonderful prepotence and superiority of the Arab blood is seen even in all those " sons of horses," testified to by the speed which has been developed in thoroughbreds which are only " sons of horses," and not " sons of mares "—*i.e.*, of pure Arab mares—and which could have been developed by no other cross.

Mr. Blunt, in his article, puts it that the Professor has inverted the hitherto admitted rôle of the Barb, which was that he was a breed brought to Barbary by the Arabs in their historic conquests and roamings, and mingled there with the less distinguished horses of Numidian antiquity. This inversion, Mr. Blunt affirms, requires better proof than any the Professor offers in the work which Mr. Blunt was criticizing.

Mr. Blunt contends that Professor Ridgeway's explanation has no probability, either local or historical, because the horses of Egypt have always been despised by the Bedouins as lacking powers of endurance and that sobriety of diet, especially in the matter of water, which is an absolute necessity of their desert existence. It is, therefore, Mr. Blunt says, to the last degree improbable that it is to Egypt the Arabs would have looked for the acquisition of brood mares and stallions. These facts, in Mr. Blunt's opinion, make the Professor's reasoning quite erroneous to those acquainted with the physical conditions.

Mr. Blunt states further that it is in Nejd alone that any extreme antiquity of horsemanship can be found; that no mention of Nejd appears, so far as he is aware, in any classic author; and that there is no reason for supposing the Kehailan, as we know him, to be otherwise than indigenous to Nejd. He recommends the Professor to make a better study of that portion of his subject which relates to Arabia if he would establish his theory on really sound ground, for Professor Ridgeway's facts are meagre and made to play a part for which they are inadequate by the ignoring of other facts far better ascertained.

In the *Century Magazine*, Mr. Osborn also disagrees with Professor Ridgeway's opinion that the Arabs never owned a good horse until they became masters of Northern Africa and secured Barbary horses. It was, he says, by reason of the wonderful excellence of their own horses that the Arabs were able to become masters of Northern Africa and to overrun all Asia to the borders of China. If the Barbary horses of those times had been as good as the Arab horses, the Arab men would never have conquered North Africa. This is what the great Abd-el-Kadir says, and there are other authorities to the same effect. The migration was from the East to the West, from Syria and Mesopotamia through Egypt to Barbary, and the horses went with the migration.

Dr. James H. Breasted, in his "History of Egypt," states that it was through the eastern corner of the Nile Valley that the prehistoric Semitic population of Asia forced their way across the dangerous deserts, while the Libyan races found entrance at the western corner, and Pharaoh's stalls boasted fine horses of Babylon. [Doubtless these were Arabian, hardly Libyan.]

I have referred to this difference of opinion between Mr. Blunt and Professor Ridgeway because many men do not trouble to think on such a subject, and if so learned and celebrated a Professor sweeps away the Arab as an Arab —a horse of Arabia—the Arab horse itself would to many minds be swept away also. On hearing that So-and-So had an Arab stallion, these persons would be prone to say: "Oh, nonsense! there are no Arab stallions, as Professor Ridgeway has shown." In which they would, of course, be wrong. They would not think about it; they would in their minds sweep away the Arab with Hipparion.

Miss Flora L. Shaw (Lady Lugard), the celebrated correspondent of the *Times*, in her book, "A Tropical Dependency," tells us that the ancient civilization of Egypt spread from South to North, which supports Mr. Blunt's view, and that of other authors, because, if Egypt were civilized from the South, it was only from Arabia that that civilization, with its horses, could have come, and a vast deal of African humanity is more or less penetrated with the blood of Arab conquerors.

CHAPTER XI

HORSES IN ANCIENT ARABIA

ALTHOUGH it is not a matter of practical importance whether or not the Arabs had horses in Arabia before Christ or before Mahomet, it is a matter of considerable interest, and I propose to give a few additional reasons in this chapter for my belief that Mr. Wildrid Blunt is right, and that the Professor is wrong, in this respect. Professor Ridgeway cites the classical authors, Strabo and Erastosthenes, as proving that the Arabs did not breed or even possess horses until the commencement of the Christian era.

I incline to the belief that the classic historians knew but very little about the interior of Arabia and comparatively little of its original history or of the original history of Assyria or Babylon, and that what they did know was mostly gossip and hearsay. Even at this day we know nothing about much of the interior of Arabia. Non-allusion to the horse in Arabia by the classic writers would prove nothing, and even if they had made statements that there were no horses in Arabia I should say that they rested upon ignorance, because the classic writers could not get into Arabia, and the Arab horses could not get out, unless taken out by the Arabs themselves, owing to the deserts. And classical literature is full of mistakes, as we now know.

The Arabs so guarded their horses, and so protected

HORSES IN ANCIENT ARABIA

their deserts, that their best horses for thousands of years have been kept, I believe, absolutely pure. The independence of the Arabians rested entirely upon the purity and superiority of their horses, which were quite as necessary to enable them to escape from their enemies after a raid as to enable them to make rapid raids into their enemies' country for loot. If their horses had not been superior to those of their enemies and of the nations around them, they never could have remained a free people.

It was the known and undoubted superiority of their horses which led the Arabs to their wonderful victories all over the world. It was not sentiment which led them to keep their mares pure and refuse to sell them. Although they greatly loved their pure-breds, their independence as a people depended on their mares. Their expression that their enemies possessed "sons of horses," but not "sons of mares," is an illustration of this. It was their mode of boasting of the purity of their mares, and therefore of their horses derived from those mares, and of expressing their scorn at their enemies for not being able to get such mares.

There was great intimacy and close connection between the Arabs and the nations more or less touching upon their borders—the Hittites, Moabites, Assyrians, Syrians, Babylonians, Phœnicians, Medes, Persians, Sabeans, Jews, Egyptians, and various other tribes—both in peace and in war, in trade, commerce, and in alliances, offensive and defensive, in battles and sieges. Most of these nations were of kindred race—Semites—and all had horses, good horses, indeed, but—again I term them so—only "sons of horses" and not "sons of mares." The following extracts which I have collected show at a glance how mixed up, so to speak, all these peoples were, and how really impossible it is to believe that the Arabs had no horses.

In a book containing an account of the Interlachen Arabian Stud, Fall River, Mass., U.S.A., Mr. Spencer Borden disputes Professor Ridgeway's contention that there were no horses in Arabia before Christ, and states that Major Upton gives definite information about the Arab horse for at least 1,500 years before Christ. He cites Rollin as quoting from " Diodorus " that Ninus in 4000 to 3500 B.C., or thereabouts, had " received powerful succours from the Arabians. His neighbours took the field with an immense cavalry." Mr. Borden adds that " no number of generations of pure blood superimposed can make an animal anything better than a mongrel."

The Arabs were always bursting out from their own country, and their enemies could practically never get in. They could only attack the fringe of the country with any chance of success, and could never hold it permanently. It is the same to this day. The Arabs, therefore, had safe breeding-places for their mares which the conquering tribes of Babylon and Assyria could not get possession of, nor could the Greeks or Romans or any other of the conquering nations, which accounts for the purity of the Arab breed.

The following occurs in 2 Esdras xv. 29 :—

" Where the nations of the dragons of Arabia shall come out with many chariots and the multitude of them shall be carried as the wind upon earth, that all they which hear them may fear and tremble."

How could the Arabians have come out with chariots unless they had had horses to draw them ? A great number of the petty nations referred to in the Bible and in the Apocrapha were more or less Arabian, and they all had horses, as the Bible shows. It was not the possession of horses for a few years only which caused the prophet Esdras to write of the Arab horses in such emphatic language.

The *Times* "Historians of the World" states that from 1225 B.C. the Arabs permitted or refused passage to the caravans of the Babylonians and the Phœnicians, and either plundered them or forced them to pay for safe passage and convoy. Pliny tells us that the Arabs cover the territory that reaches from the Euphrates to Egypt, and that every man among them was a warrior, and that on their camels and swift horses they are everywhere to be seen. . . . Both in attack and defence nothing could touch them because of this fleetness of their horses. Pliny's words are worthy of note: "Camels and swift horses." He would scarcely have used the words "swift horses" in this collocation of words if the Arabs had not had fleet horses for a considerable period. He speaks of their swift horses as a well-known fact and a matter of course.

In the "Naturalist History of the Bible," H. B. Tristram says that "Resch," translated in our version "dromedary," really means a high-bred horse, and many examples are given. If so, and if the animals translated dromedaries were really high-bred horses, what becomes of the Professor's argument? I am no Hebrew scholar, but I vote for the high-bred horses.

This history tells us also that in pre-Islamitic times the great yearly fair and gathering was held at Okad, only a day's journey from Mecca. It was a national meeting, frequented by men of all conditions from all quarters of the Arab Peninsula; and horse-races, athletic games, poetical recitals, and every kind of public amusement diversified the more serious commercial transactions of an open fair. One might well ask how could there have been horse-races there in the pre-Islamitic times if the Arabs had them not?

The same authority mentions also that in 587 B.C. Nebuchadnezzar led a military expedition against the Bedouins of Kedar and the Arab tribes which had settled to the east of Palestine, and that the town of Teredon was founded by Nebuchadnezzar at this time as a bulwark against the Bedouins and to check their incursions. This was necessary because, as I before stated, the Arabs could get out practically whenever they chose, although the enemy could not get in. Some of the outer country was of the richest in the world, with feed everywhere. Much of the inner country was largely barren, and only the Arabs knew how to get to where feed and water were to be found, or had horses with hardihood sufficient to reach it. Professor Sayce, for instance, writes : " The Arabian King provided water for the Assyrian army in its march across the desert."

The history goes on to say that Sapor of Persia zealously devoted himself to the task of keeping the rapacious Bedouins out of civilized regions, which was a very serious problem for the rulers of countries bordering on the desert.

Reference is further made to Ammianus Marcellinus, who states that the Arabs cover the territory from the Euphrates to Egypt; that every man among them is a warrior ; and that on their camels and swift, fine-limbed horses they are everywhere to be seen. It points out that the position of Arabia between the river valley of the Nile, the Euphrates and the Tigris brought the Arabs, who were continually wandering about, into close connection with Egypt and Babylon, and that the wandering herdsmen had need of corn, tools, weapons ; the Egyptians and Babylonians of horses, camels, skins, and wool. Here " horses " are put first. How can it be maintained that these Arabs had no horses ?

Startling proof of the difficulty of entering Arabia appears in an Adelaide daily paper of November 20, 1909, which gives an account of a recent attempt at exploration in Southern Arabia by two Englishmen,

Messrs. Bury and Gethin, in order to visit the buried cities known to exist there. They obtained an escort of fifteen men and eight camels at the fishing village of Irka, but they were stopped by the Bedouins the day after starting. All their goods were taken away from them, they were shot at for fun, were ignominously sent back to the coast, and narrowly escaped with their lives. So it ever was from the beginning. No one could get in without the Arabs' permission.

The *Adelaide Express* of March 5, 1910, reports an account of another recent adventure with the Bedouins in unexplored Arabia, given by Mr. Douglas Carruthers to the members of the Royal Geographical Society. He told the Society that during the past quarter of a century knowledge of the interior of Arabia had not increased in any way, although it still possessed the largest tract of unknown country in the world. While watering camels at a well, the speaker said that he and his companion were called upon to " stand and deliver " by four Bedouins ; and, if they had not had a man of that tribe with them, they would probably have lost their camels and been left stranded in the desert. He found at this very well the ruined remains of a large Khan caravansera. Such a building as this, far away out in the sterile desert, must denote an ancient prosperity which had long disappeared, as, indeed, is also proved by the ruined cities.

The *Times* " History," referred to above, quotes a writer who says of the Arabs that that nation were lovers of liberty, never admitting of any foreign Prince, for, Arabia being partly desert, it could not be subdued, and so Ninus, the Assyrian King, obtained the assistance of the Prince of Arabia to invade Babylon, and Ninus sent the Prince of Arabia back into his own country with many rich spoils.

The same work relates that Alexander the Great,

when at the mouth of the Euphrates, took precautions to prevent Arabia from becoming entirely inaccessible, since he contemplated making himself master of that country. The Arab horses rendered it impossible for Alexander to carry out his desire, and his early death effectually stopped his taking the desired precautions.

It also tells us that from 2500 B.C. the Arabs had trade with Egypt and Babylon, obtaining corn, tools, and weapons from the Egyptians and Babylonians in exchange for the horses, camels, and skins and wool of the Arabs. Where did those horses which the history refers to —" horses of the Arabs "—come from ? It puts the Arabs as selling-owners of horses. They could not have had them to sell if they had not bred them. However much the Egyptians at some early period of their history might have wanted horses, because they had none of their own, that could not be said of the Babylonians, who had huge armies of cavalry. What the Babylonians wanted to trade for was *Arab* horses—" sons of mares "—which they could not get except from the Arabs. They did not want horses, speaking generally " sons of horses." The neighbouring countries were crowded with ordinary horses, very excellent horses undoubtedly, but as undoubtedly inferior to the horses of the Arabs : only " sons of horses," and not " sons of mares."

We learn from the same source that in 701 B.C. King Hezekiah was shut up by Sennacherib in Jerusalem like a bird in its cage, but that the town had a good garrison, and Hezekiah had faithful troops and had enlisted a number of Arabian soldiers. King Hezekiah would have been very unlikely to have enlisted Arabian soldiers if they had not had horses, and without horses it would have been very difficult for these Arab soldiers to have got to Jerusalem to be hired, " shut up " as it was by Sennacherib.

It also says that, thanks to the accumulation of recent evidence, the most ardent partisans of Hebrew records now vie with one another in tracing back the evidences of civilization in Egypt and Mesopotamia by centuries and by millenia to 6000 to 7000 B.C. I will not believe that it was possible that under such circumstances the whole world surrounding Arabia could be swarming with horses, and that the Arabs, the cleverest, the bravest, and most intellectual of all the Semitic peoples, should not have any in their own country. It would have been a miracle.

According to the same authority, the oldest known copy of the Bible dates from the fourth century A.D.— 1000 years after the last Syrian records were made and read and buried and forgotten, and the Mesopotamian records date back some 5000—perhaps 7000—years B.C.

The remains of magnificent structures in Arabia go far towards confirming what Arab tradition tells us of the glories of ancient times. Besides these, there are other authorities, some of which I have quoted, which go to prove the antiquity of the Arabian horse. They are, however, so intermingled with information bearing on other matters that I have not deemed it necessary to repeat them in this chapter. But one authority I must quote, which I came across after nearly every word of this book was written.

I have already said that in my opinion the classic authors knew nothing about the interior of Arabia, so that their authority, cited by Professor Ridgeway, amounts to very little. The book which has just come to my notice is entitled, " The Conquest of Syria, Persia, and Egypt by the Saracens," by the Rev. Simon Ockley, M.A., Vicar of Swaresey, Cambridgeshire, 1708, collected from the most authentic Arabic authors, especially manuscripts not hitherto published in any European language, many of them from the invaluable collection of Archbishop Laud.

Mr. Ockley tells us that "the Arabians were a people as little taken notice of by the Greek and Roman authors as could well be supposed, considering their nearness." He blames the Greek writers for not giving a just account of the Arabians, and quotes the words of "an ingenious author" who was well aware of the imperfections of the Greeks, and who said in his book, A.D. 637, that the Greeks are justly to be censured for their succinctness and obscurity on this subject. In showing the ignorance of these Greek authors, Mr. Ockley expressly approves of a saying of the "ingenious author." "What lame accounts must we then expect from those who compile histories of the Saracens out of the Byzantine historians?" Mr. Ockley, in short, puts it that those Greek authors who knew anything about Arabia had too much other business to trouble to write about it, while those who knew very little about it made a mess of their work. He sneers at the Byzantine authors for their mistaken notions about "that learned, copious, and elegant language," the Arabic, which he describes as too difficult for the Greek writers to understand; and he says that these had a want of due information, and therefore a wrong opinion, of the Arabians, who before Mahomet's time were idolaters, always a warlike people, seldom at peace with one another or their neighbours, and their chief excellency consisted in breeding and managing horses. He returns frequently to the Greeks later on in the book, and again denounces the Byzantine authors and "those other writers who have followed them blindfold in their account of Mahomet." He concludes that, as for Byzantines, their authority in this matter is of no great weight at all.

Mr. Ockley is supported by J. Morgan in his "History of Algiers," 1728, who states that Pliny complained of their insufficiency, and adds: "As for the Greeks, Pausanius says their knowledge was little or nothing." To the same effect writes Professor Sayce in his "Ancient Empires of the East." He says : " We must give up our faith in the legends of a later age, and must turn from the great writers of Greece and Rome as unsafe guides."

Mr. Ockley sets out the text of part of the letter mentioned in my former book, whereby the owners of pure Arab horses at the battle of Damascus were given double share of spoil, to which he adds that some were not at first satisfied, but upon appeal to Omar he confirmed the order, as the Prophet had done the same after the battle of Chaiban.

After I had discovered Mr. Ockley, I dipped into Professor Maspero's "The Struggle of the Nations," edited by Professor Sayce, to see if I could find anything bearing upon the dispute between Professor Ridgeway and Mr. Wilfrid Blunt, and I find in a note (5) at p. 30 that Strabo appears in one place at least to have taken his information from Aristobulos, whose stories " should always be taken with caution." A note on the same page shows how credulous was "Monsieur" Aristobulus, who stated that in summer snakes cannot cross the streets without running the risk of being literally baked by the sun. At p. 47, Maspero speaks of a great Elamite empire whose existence was " vaguely " hinted at by the Greeks, and at p. 63 tells us that the Phœnician tradition of the exodus of an inexhaustible population from Arabia was misunderstood by Herodotus. These extracts, without searching through the very learned Maspero's work, go to show that Mr. Ockley and Mr. Blunt are right in not relying on the Greeks, although one can but think that much more authority to the same effect could be dug out if you deeply dived into Maspero. But it is not necessary ; I have said enough.

The *Times*, in a leading article on November 1, 1910, reminds us that the Greek dramatists in treating old stories never insist upon their ancient and unfamiliar circumstances, and tells us that it was an Egyptian priest who said to Solon that " you Greeks are all children; you know nothing of your own past." The article adds that through their lack of memory they had little sense of the vivid strangeness of the past and none of an older civilization than their own. How remarkably the Egyptian priest and the quaint old Church of England priest, and the " ingenious author " of A.D. 637, agree with one another in ridiculing the statements of the Greeks on this subject!

Mr. C. M. Doughty published in 1908 an abridgment of his very great book, " Travels in Arabia Deserta," over which he wandered for a great number of years, and no book that I know of so plainly reveals the truth and depicts the interior.

Plain facts are calmly stated, and bring home to one's mind as one reads the reason why it was impossible for the Assyrians and other great conquering nations to conquer Arabia.

For many years he was daily in danger of his life, and takes little note of horses.

Incidentally, however, he mentions that the Gulf horses, bred in the river countries, although of good stature and swift, are not esteemed by the " inner " Arabs; that " their own daughters of the desert are worth five of the other, which are very sure of foot to climb in rocky ground, and are good weight-carriers." He was told that one of their mares could carry four men.

Mr. Doughty's simple tale brought before my mind the most eloquent and touching wail in all literature—that of St. Paul, who had travelled in Arabia. I would I had space to insert it (2 Cor. xi. 23).

Job's glorious description of the Arab horse a thousand years before the Christian era, the wail of St. Paul at its commencement who had travelled in Arabia, and the unspeakable contempt shown by the Arabs for the self-sufficient Englishmen of whom a few months ago they made targets because they entered into their deserts (so as, however, not to kill them), all bear witness to the Arab's unchangeableness. What Maxims and Field Artillery may do in the future has yet to be learned. Even, notwithstanding these, the Bedouins in December, 1910, seized Keran from the Turks and held it for a while.

Mr. Doughty tells us that the best brood-mares of pure blood, which are few, are each valued in the Arab tribes at twenty-five camels. He relates that he saw a mare stabling herself in the midday shadow of the master's booth, approach the sitters, and put down her soft nose; they turned their heads to kiss her, till the sheik rose to scold her away. Wild and dizzy camels are daily seen, but seldom impetuous horses, and perverse never; the most, he says, are of a bay colour.

CHAPTER XII

AN OUTLINE SKETCH OF SOME EASTERN HISTORY

RECENT research has brought to light whole libraries of the Kings of Assyria, Egypt, Babylon, and other kindred nations, and their monuments, proclamations and traditions carry us back eight or ten milleniums, so that we have better knowledge of the peoples of Egypt, Mesopotamia, and Arabia than we have of the peoples of the British Islands in the days of Cæsar. We know very much more of Nebuchadnezzar and also of Queen Esther than we do of Boadicea, Queen of the Iceni.

A writer in *Harper's Monthly*, May, 1905, states that from the quaternary epoch the Arabian deserts have been inhabited, and, in " Monument Facts," Professor Sayce says that an active correspondence existed in the Egyptian Foreign Office with the Governors and vassal Princes in Canaan and Syria, as well as with the Kings of Babylonia, Assyria, Mesopotamia, and Asia Minor. He points out, for the information of those " very superior persons who deny everything," that research is constantly demonstrating how dangerous it is to question or deny the veracity of tradition or of an ancient record until we know all the facts. I am not learned enough in these modern controversies to hazard a guess as to whether the one Professor would put his brother Professor amongst the " very superior persons who deny everything," and I admire the great grasp and ability of Professor Ridgeway's book; but, as I said before, I cannot believe but that he is mistaken about horses not being in Arabia before Christ. Sir Thomas Holdich, in "The Gates of India," says that it is always best to assume in the first instance that a local tradition firmly held and strongly asserted has a basis of fact to support it.

Professor Delitzsch's "Babel and Bible" has a picture of King Assur-bani-pal (Sardanapalus) at the hunt riding a most beautifully formed horse, without stirrups, the reins on the horse's neck, and shooting with bow and arrow. There is another picture of the same king lion hunting, thrusting his spear down the lion's throat. Those are almost pictures of the pure Arab horses of to-day. How many thoroughbreds would so face a lion?

In the "Exodus of Israel," T. R. Birks says that the construction of terraces and dykes preserved a supply of water and soil, and made Yemen centuries before Moses the paradise of Arabia, and laid the foundation for a mighty empire, which disappeared from the earth when the dams were broken through. There is authentic evidence of this, he says, in the inscriptions lately discovered. I would ask, can it be conceived that this mighty Empire had no horses? I maintain that it is inconceivable.

Colonel Reignier Conder, in "Syrian Stone Lore," writes that in the ninth year of Assur-bani-pal, 639 B.C., there was an Arab invasion of Syria. Could that have been done without horses?

In "Nineveh and its Remains," Layard says that the horses represented in the Assyrian sculptures appear to be of noble breed, and that Assyria was celebrated for its own horses then as it is to this day. Layard not only says that Assyria was celebrated for its horses, but that it was "celebrated for the noblest breeds of Arabia." Layard's words would be utterly out of place if there had been no horses in Arabia, and show that the Assyrians were as anxious as other tribes to get Arab horses.

William Youatt states that a few wild horses were yet to be seen on some of the deserts of Arabia, which are hunted by the Bedouins for their flesh. I think that it may be doubtful whether wild horses were in existence in Arabia so recently as Youatt's time; still, he must have got the information from some apparently reliable authority. Undoubtedly there were, I think, wild horses in Arabia at some time, and, if there were, how can it be contended that it had no horses at all? I do not propose to dwell on this, but it may very well be that these wild horses were the source of the celebrated horses of Nejd.

In the *Contemporary Review*, Emil Reich says that the Babylonians and the Hebrews both come from Arabia, which was the "store chamber of nations," and that that gifted people (the Arabs) emigrated in all directions thousands of years before Christ. Thus, the Babylonians, the Hebrews, the Masai, and probably many other unknown tribes in Persia, Afghanistan, Beluchistan, and India still preserve the Arab legends. In fact, Mesopotamia, on the borders of Arabia, was the centre of the commerce and civilization of the ancient world, in all of which the Arabs took a leading part. It seems to me impossible that they had no horses in Arabia, when all around the Arabs up to their very borders the ground shook and resounded "with the stamping of their hoofs," and they themselves fought for centuries both allied with and against armies using horses. To suppose that the Arabs had no horses before Christ is to suppose them born fools instead of the most intellectual race then on earth.

In "Eclipse and O'Kelly," Theodore Andrea Cooke, author also of "A History of the English Turf," states that the Darley Arabian was a pure representative of the oldest and best indigenous breed of horses in the world, and that that was the reason why the blood of the Darley Arabian proved itself so potent. How far "indigenous" it is not necessary to inquire, but Mr. Cooke's opinion clearly is that it has been a pure breed for a very lengthened period, and that otherwise the blood could not be so prepotent.

He suggests that the breed was indigenous in Nejd in Arabia many a century before the Koran was ever written. Then, inspired by his subject, he says that it was the breed which made Pindar sing of Cyrene, the city of fair steeds and goodly riders; which gave Carthage in 1400 B.C. the crest of horses' heads upon her coins, and furnished those Numidian steeds that helped Hannibal to teach Romans the value of cavalry. It was the same breed that helped to spread the faith of the Prophet so widely and victoriously over the face of the earth, and gave William the Conqueror his victorious cavalry at Hastings.

He thinks that the Keheilan or Arabian was the original type from which both Barb and Turk were easily derivatives, and that it was from the East and not from the West that Ancient Egypt took her best breed, as England took it later on. Nejd, he adds, offers, in fact, very much the same facilities for horse forage as are found on the principal horse-breeding plateaus of Central Asia. He observes that the points of the Arabian horse are so persistent throughout the artistic record of its life-history that there is probably very little difference between the best of Mr. Wilfrid Blunt's Arabs to-day and their far-off progenitors who carried the first horsemen of the Prophet on their military Evangel throughout Africa, Asia, and Europe.

In the *Pall Mall Magazine*, January, 1905, Mr. R. N. Hall states that " Saba " in South Arabia was a world-power long prior to the time of King Solomon, and a rival to Egypt in power, influence, arts, culture, literature, and civilization, and provided the basis of the Phoenician alphabet, the mother of all our Eastern systems. I contend that it is impossible that such a world-power had no horses.

Mr. James Robertson, in his " Beginning of the Hebrew History," states that there was an intimate relation between Arabia and Babylonia in the third millennium B.C., and that the dynasty of Hammurabi, a great Babylonian king, is now generally admitted to have been Arabian in origin.

In " The First of Empires," Mr. W. St. Chad Boscawen says that the annual war no doubt had its origin in the tribal raid of the Arabs, and that Babylon had furnished no line of kings until the rise of a dynasty of Arab rulers.

In the " Sacred City of the Ethiopians," Mr. Theodore Bent writes that the inscriptions place the Sabœans of Arabia by incontrovertible documentary evidence in the heart of Abyssinia as early as the seventh or eighth century B.C., and that the numerous early Arabian inscriptions which we have establish the fact that the Ethiopians' origin as well as their written script came from Arabia. These Sabœans must have had horses.

Mr. Bent also quotes Ludolphus as saying that Ethiopians are not natives of the land, but came out of Arabia, and that an Arabian colony settled on the coast at a very remote period, and had a strong fortified town at Yeha or Ava, which he says is absolutely proved by the mass of Hunyaritic inscriptions found there.

In " Human Origins," Mr. S. Laing describes the Tablet of Suefura at Waddy Magerah, which shows the king conquering an Arabian enemy, as being 6,000 years old, and he puts the Hyksos as mainly nomad tribes of Arabia. He says that before the days of Mohammet, Arabia was a land of culture and literature, a seat of powerful kingdoms and wealthy commerce, and that in the eighth century B.C. the Arabian frontiers extended to those of Nineveh, and that it was then an ancient kingdom. He also says that the recent Arabian discoveries disclose not only a civilized and commercial kingdom at a remote antiquity, but a literary world at a date comparable to that of the Egyptian hieroglyphics, and long prior to the oldest known inscription in Phœnician characters. Further, that the horse must have been known at a very early period in Chaldæa, for Sargon, in 3800 B.C., rode in brazen chariots over rugged mountains, which make it the more singular that the horse should have been unknown in Egypt and Arabia, for it must have been introduced almost the very first moment when trading caravans arrived. Of course, everyone would think so, and I contend that they thought rightly, and that it must have been as Mr. Laing says. It would have been quite impossible for the Arabs to have done what they did without horses.

In "A Journey through the Yemen," Mr. W. B. Harris says the Ancient Egyptians owed the foundation of their arts and learning to the inhabitants of Southern Arabia, . . . that a remarkable state of civilization and commerce is found to have existed there contemporaneously with early Egyptian times. What was wrongly believed to have been a country of savagery has been proved to have contained a cultured population skilled in arts and excelling in commerce, and many of the recently discovered inscriptions in the Yemen date from a period contemporary with Egpytian hieroglyphics.

Mr. W. H. Flower, C.B., in "The Horse: a Study in Natural History," says that horses were imported from Asia through Greece and Italy for the purpose of improving the races of Europe throughout the whole of the historic period. Although it will be certain that those horses were "Eastern horses," horses more or less largely crossed with Arab blood, "sons of horses," it must be admitted to have been utterly impossible to have obtained such numbers of "sons of mares"—*i.e.*, pure Arab stallions—in fact, we know that most of these imports were not "sons of mares."

In his "Egypt and Babylon," the Rev. George Rawlinson says that Schweinfurth seems to prove that Arabia was the original connecting link between Egypt and Babylonia, that the Phœnicians came from Arabia, and that Babylonian and Assyrian inscriptions supply information about Arabia from about 3000 B.C. Recent discoveries go very much further back.

Dr. Fritz Hummel, in "The Ancient Hebrew Tradition," states that the ancient Hebrews were Arabs, and that an Arabian dynasty occupied the throne of Babylon in the time of Abraham. The ritual language of the Old Testament, he says, can only be explained by Babylonian and other dialects through Arabic. In early Babylon, about 3000 B.C., King Gudei was the head of a confederacy of which Arabia was a part, and the Arabs gave new life to the effete civilization of Babylon, represented by mighty buildings and numerous inscriptions. Egypt and Babylonia, the two most ancient civilized states of the world, fell a prey to the Arabs. The Assyrians themselves were of Arab blood.

In "Bible Problems," Professor Cheyne contends that the Assyrian inscriptions refer to North Arabian regions near the South Border of Palestine, named Musri and Kus; that Abraham did not go down to Egypt, but to Misrion, North Arabia; and that Solomon did not marry a daughter of the King of Egypt, but of Misrion. The horses which Solomon bought were not from Egypt—they had no pastures to breed in there—but from North Arabia. This was many hundreds of years before Mahommet.

Professor Hummel, in "The Ancient Hebrew," says that according to tradition the desert region to the east of the Lower Tigris, and also part of South Babylonia, were from the very earliest times the resort of a race of nomads, who must have originally come from Arabia, and that it is manifest that for countless ages there must have been brisk intercourse between Arabia and the nations on its frontiers.

In "Explorations in the Bible Lands," H. V. Hilprecht states that the Babylonian and Assyrian inscriptions supply information on several parts of Arabia from about 3000 B.C., and that an Arabian dynasty ruled at Babylon at the time of Abraham. He also says that Arabia was the original home of all the Semites, and that even the Patriarch Jacob was regarded simply as an Aramean. Professor Sayce regards the Book of Job as really a Hebrew adoption of a remnant of Arab literature.

SOME EASTERN HISTORY

George Rawlinson, in his "Phœnicia," tells us that Phœnicia was more or less intimately connected with the Assyrians, Babylonians, Syrians, Hebrews, Moabites, Edomites, and Arabs. All these, except on Professor Ridgeway's theory of the Arabs, had horses. How can it be supposed that they would not have horses also? Rawlinson also says that the chariots of Assyria in the days of Assur-bani-pal were drawn by horses of great strength and swiftness. They are thus described by the prophet Isaiah: "Their horses' hoofs shall be counted like flint, and their wheels like a whirlwind." Everyone knows that the Arab horse is wonderfully strong for his size. Rawlinson mentions further that Alexander the Great suffered losses from the attacks of the neighbouring Arabs, and that the expression of the horses' heads in the sculptures recently discovered have a finish that is absolute perfection.

In his "Parthia," also, Rawlinson tells us that the bulk of the Parthian cavalry was of the lightest and most agile description. The rider could use his weapons with equal ease and effect whether his horse was stationary or at full gallop, or whether he was advancing towards or hurriedly retreating from the enemy. As compared with these troops, the Romans were thoroughly inferior both in respect of number and of excellence. Clouds of Parthian horses hung upon the retreating columns, and destroyed those who could not keep up with the main body.

A cutting from the *World's News*, forwarded me by an unknown correspondent, says that the purest of all Arab horses are the Kochlain, whose genealogy has been preserved for over 2,000 years.

CHAPTER XIII

A WORD OR TWO CONCERNING REVERSION

I HAVE no intention of writing, and I disclaim having the competence to write, a scientific dissertation on reversion; but a few words on the subject from those who do understand it will be useful to my farming friends. The quotations will tend to show both why the Arab is so perfect and the thoroughbred so much the contrary.

Mr. Cooke, in the *Cornhill Magazine* of June, 1908, writes that if it had not been for Eastern blood we should never have had English horses worth the name at all. The English thoroughbred, as we proudly call him, is neither wholly English nor wholly thoroughbred, and will soon, he fears, even more completely justify a parallel with Voltaire's cruel phrase about the holy Roman Empire. He cites Professor Ridgeway himself as pointing out that the acquisition of horses by the Arabs was one of the most momentous events in history, for from that day the breed was fostered and developed on the tableland of the Nejd in a manner that no other nation of horse-lovers has ever surpassed, and the Arabian foray horses soon became a power.

Fry's Magazine, July, 1908, says that there is uncertainty associated with the breeding and racing of the thoroughbred: amazing uncertainty. The romance of the turf is largely made up of a gamble in yearlings, of high-priced failures, and low-priced successes.

CONCERNING REVERSION

The *Australasian*, of January 1, 1907, says: "It is impossible always completely to eliminate a foreign strain; a reappearance of the characteristic of a foreign breed 100 years after it was introduced has been known."

From the *Sydney Mail* of July 3, 1907: "You can get two stallions of almost identical blood, but absolutely different in type. Woe be to the mare that is mated to a sire of the same family with a marked different type. In their progeny will be exaggerated all the faults and blemishes of the family." I might fortify that by referring to the union of negro and Caucasian blood, in which I learned over seventy years ago that the offspring generally showed the faults of both races, and but little of the virtue of either—a belief which governs all Australia with passion at the present moment.

In an article in the *Geographical Journal*, September, 1907, on "Journeys in North Mesopotamia," it was stated that "the Arab is proud of his mare's blood for its own sake. He will show you a broken-down little crock, and inform you with perfect truth that she is of the best blood in the Jayirah. He prefers and admires the bad-looking thoroughbred to the finest made cross-breed." All history and all breeding show that he is right. "It is the blood that tells." How often has that been said and demonstrated in our English history!

A cavalry officer in the Austrian Service states that "the stud at Kisber is entirely of English blood, but they would not buy half-bred English mares however good-looking for this stud, because they could not depend on their back blood, and were afraid of their progeny throwing back to the cart or under-bred horse, and so proving soft and slow."

R. H. Lock, in his book on "Heredity and Evolution," says that "reversion leads to the appearance in the offspring of a character which was not visibly present in either parent."

Darwin affirms that a character derived from a distinct cross after having disappeared during one or several generations will suddenly reappear, children constantly resembling in appearance or disposition one of their grandparents or some more distant relation.

I took an extract from an author (I think Darwin himself), which says that " neither in the case of a breed contaminated by a single cross, nor when half-bred animals have been matched together during many generations, can it be said how soon the tendency to reversion will be obliterated, and that this is an essential part of the principle of inheritance."

In Sir Humphrey de Trafford's great book, T. H. Weehman lays it down that " the purer the race of the parent the more certainty there is of its transmitting its qualities to the offspring," which accounts for the success of the pure-bred Arab sire. But, mind, he must be pure.

In " Eclipse and O'Kelly," it is stated that " the one or more white feet are still repeated in the famous descendants of Eclipse that have made their mark in English racing. Sires are known to have been crossed with Barb blood when used as war-horses in mediæval times."

Lord Egerton of Tatton, in the *National Review*, June, 1905, says that " the larger a horse the more difficult to rear, and the more subject to a variety of defects which constitute unsoundness." The six inches which the thoroughbred has gained in height since the Stud Book was started would possibly therefore alone account for his delicacy and softness.

The *Times* of March 15, 1907, in an account of a show, says that " the hunter sires were not strong numerically or as regards quality, and so far as the past can teach us a lesson there must be absolutely pure blood on one side of the horse. A Stud Book sire might beget good hunting stock from a thoroughbred mare, but even this mode of mating is not always satisfactory."

CONCERNING REVERSION

The following extracts are from the *Australasian*:

May 12, 1906.—" All experience goes to show that inbred horses make the best sires, and are able to perpetuate their line better than crossbred horses." I add that the inbreeding must be of pure blood only.

July 28, 1906.—" The great stock-breeders of old relied greatly on inbreeding, and proved conclusively that properly exercised inbreeding has no bad effect. Since then scientific men generally have adopted the opinion of the old-world farmers."

May 5, 1907.—" I would place more reliance on the opinions of the experienced husbandman than of that of the most able veterinary surgeon. The former is generally a keen observer of all the phenomena of the breeding of domestic animals, while the latter has devoted all his attention to the causes and the nature of disease."

June 1, 1907.—" Mendel's law in cross-breeding is referred to in the *Journal of the Royal Agricultural Society*, England, by Mr. R. H. Biffen, who says that in crossbreeding in the second generation there is a tendency to revert to one or other of the original types. When two widely distinct breeds are crossed, the characteristics of each breed appear in a very mixed manner in the progeny."

July 6, 1907.—" That there is a great element of luck in horse-breeding is demonstrated in the origin of Gallinule and Pioneer."

August 31, 1907.—" In all the extreme crosses the produce are very uneven and generally disappointing. Occasionally one meets with a remarkably good horse bred in this way, but they are the rare exceptions. The right description of thoroughbred as a sire for raising remounts is getting rare. They have for a long time been bred for the one purpose—speed, and every other good quality has been neglected to obtain speed. The thoroughbred horse has degenerated during the last half century." In South Africa I heard of many instances of Australian horses doing wonderful work, and the majority of them were by Arab sires. They were low set, with well-sprung ribs, and legs like steel.

November 9, 1907.—" Within the last quarter of a century several instances of horned horses have occurred in Great Britain, and oddly enough with one exception they appeared among thoroughbreds." (I think that the word "naturally" should be substituted for "oddly," because the thoroughbred is the most mixed breed in England.)

" In India the Australian breeder has a market which his English cousin had not, and Mr. Weir advises the building up of a foundation stock of mares by means of Arab and Welsh pony blood."

"Horse-breeding in England and India, and Army Horses Abroad," by Sir Walter Gilbey, Bart., tells us that " it is well known that in the breeding of every species of animal the endeavour to obtain one quality often produces manifest deterioration in other attributes. Such has been the consequence of aiming solely at speed in the horse ; other essentials, such as strength and endurance, have been in great measure lost. The author of 'English Racers and Saddle Horses in the Past and Present Centuries' declared that at that date (1836) there were powerful reasons for concluding that the single quality of speed possessed by the modern racer is a bad substitute for the fine old union of speed, stoutness, and structural power possessed by the old racer. Saxons and Danes brought horses of various breeds into England, the most useful of which were of Eastern breeds. William the Conqueror brought with him many Spanish horses. William himself at Hastings rode a Spanish horse."

The man who has devoted himself exclusively to the production of one class of horse cannot rid himself of the prejudices he has necessarily formed. The modern race-horse—superior as he is in point of speed to his ancestors of a hundred and fifty years ago—is wanting in those qualities which would fit him as the sire of useful horses. That is like one of the immutable laws of

CONCERNING REVERSION

mechanics, that what you gain in speed you lose in power.

"The King himself" (I have lost the reference, but I think Henry VIII.) "lent support to the turf, keeping at Hampton Court a grey Arab stallion, whose services were available for mares at a stated fee."

In "Three Voyages of a Naturalist," Mr. M. J. Nicol writes that the Pitcairners resemble their ancestors, the *Bounty* mutineers, every alternate generation. This is interesting evidence, because apparently indifferently written without any regard to Darwin or his laws, or to thoroughbred or Arab horses.

F. W. Headley, in "Life and Evolution," says that our domesticated animals have not the health of the wild stocks. The zebra's health is as rude and strong as his temper. The high-bred horse compared with him is a hothouse plant, and this regrettable fact we must attribute largely to the softening of the environment.

CHAPTER XIV

THE THOROUGHBRED

I NOW propose to say something more about the thoroughbred, and, if his admirers will kindly honour me by reading the facts herein put together, they will perhaps admit that there is much which deserves their serious consideration.

Some thoughtless persons, and many who are otherwise, believe that the word "thoroughbred" signifies a horse of pure breed: an erroneous belief, which is encouraged by certain people of influence. That is not at all the meaning of the word and never was, yet it has been so frequently asserted that it is almost currently believed. Even Mr. Homer Davenport, the celebrated American breeder, writes that "thoroughbred" meant a horse of pure desert Arabian blood on sire's and dam's side, imported into England and bred there. That is incorrect.

The true meaning is that the horse has sufficient breeding of a recognized sort to be entered in the Stud Book; in other words, he is thoroughly enough bred on certain lines to claim entry in it. What the exact breeding really was, when the Stud Book was first published, nowhere appears and nobody knows, nor can it be ever known. In fact, no horse ever entered in the Stud Book except an Arab was of pure breed. The best horses in England except Arabs were undoubtedly of greatly mixed breed

THE THOROUGHBRED 135

when the Stud Book was started, and have been of mixed breed ever since, and continue so to this day. I think it would be safe to say that there was 60 or 70 per cent. of Arab blood in it, and probably more, because it began by entering only "horses of note"—*i.e.*, horses of note as racers—and all the best of the racing horses of note were largely of Arab blood. The thoroughbred other than the pure Arabs was never pure. It was mixed blood on both sire's and dam's side, and is so still. This is proved by the Stud Book itself.

Prior to 1793 there was no Stud Book. In that year, Mr. J. Weatherby, junior, compiled the first Stud Book, of which I have an original copy now before me. Its title-page is as follows :

"The General Stud Book, containing (with few exceptions) the Pedigrees of every horse, mare, etc., of note, that has appeared on the Turf, for the last fifty years, with many of an earlier date : together with some account of the Foreign horses and mares from whence is derived the present breed of racers in Great Britain and Ireland. London. Printed by H. Reynell, No. 21, Piccadilly, for J. Weatherby, junior, No. 7, Oxenden Street, near the Hay-market. MDCCXCIII."

Two facts appear by this title-page: first, that it is not pretended that every horse of note was entered ; secondly, that it does not appear of what breeding or blood were the horses which actually were entered, except of the Arabs named in it, which are many.

I have a subsequent volume by Mr. James Weatherby, of which the title-page is shorter—namely :

"The General Stud Book, containing Pedigrees of race-horses, etc., from the Restoration to the present time. London. Printed for James Weatherby, 7, Oxenden Street, near the Hay-market, by Henry Reynell, 21, Piccadilly, near the Black Bear, 1803." This record purports to go back further than the earlier book—viz., to the Restoration—but, as that was more than a hundred years earlier than the Stud Book, the information must have been greatly hearsay. For all that, the Stud Book tells us the horses entered in it, except Arabs, may have been only two or three removes from cart horses. Most people believe, as I believe, that it was otherwise, but that belief is not founded on actual knowledge, and is not obtained from the book but from tradition.

Mr. Alfred E. T. Watson, in the *Badminton Magazine*, November, 1907, shows this, and writes that " the history of the turf about the middle of the last century (the eighteenth) was confusing, because there were no registrations of ownership, and for various reasons, sometimes indefinite, men ran their horses in all sorts of names."

Professor Ewart states that there are several Occidental and several African and Oriental varieties in our British breeds of horses, and that the thoroughbred is a mixture of African and Oriental varieties, including amongst its ancestors several wild species, and is a breed of multiple origin.

What is a mongrel? Webster puts it as " of a mixed breed, hybrid : anything of mixed breed." " Hybrid " he defines as a " mongrel plant or animal ; the produce of a female plant or animal which has been impregnated by a male of a different variety, species, or germs." That description exactly defines the thoroughbred horse. Therefore the thoroughbred is really a mongrel, and he can never be anything else, because he is a mongrel on both sides ; both sires and dams are of mixed breed—greatly mixed, as Professor Ewart shows. Some enthusiasts, anxious to insure a place amongst " the upper ten " for the thoroughbred, say that after a cross has been mated with pure blood for six or eight generations, the mongrel blood is bred out. That is not so. Reversion

THE THOROUGHBRED

may always come in; but here there is no such mating: both sides are crossbred. If you cross a mulatto with white blood indefinitely you may probably breed out the black blood, subject, of course, to reversion; but if you breed mulatto with mulatto for ever, you will get nothing but mulattos, subject equally, of course, to reversion. So with the thoroughbreds: both sires and dams are like mulattos—*i.e.*, of mixed blood—and mixed blood bred in and in for ever will never become pure but will be always mixed.

Nature, April, 1908, in order to prove this with regard to cattle, refers to a phenomenon which may be interesting to naturalists, but alarming to breeders of shorthorn cattle—viz., that the roan shorthorn is a hybrid and must remain so for ever. These last six words, "and must remain so for ever," are as applicable to the thoroughbred as to the roan shorthorn, and are true of all animal life. I cite this the more willingly because it cannot be said that there is any Arab or thoroughbred prejudice in the writer, who is not referring to horses but to shorthorn cattle.

The relative merits of the two breeds—*i.e.*, the Arab and the thoroughbred—have been judged by the capacity of the thoroughbred after nearly two centuries of breeding for speed only, and with long training, much coddling in warm stables, abundance of physic, often with blinkers, always with rugs, and frequently with tubes down their throats, to outrun the Arab on a fast gallop for a short race during a very short life. Hence, most thoroughbreds are weeds and begetters of weeds. But such a training and such a test is not a fair test, nor does it give a just measure of the true excellence of a horse or of a breed for general usefulness.

An Arab gentleman, or a Bedouin of the desert, or a Turkish or Persian Pasha, or a cavalry officer, would scoff at you if you were to tell him that he should test a horse for the practical purposes of life by any such breeding or training. The Arab horse has his rider on his back often all day long, and not infrequently all night, too, in terrible country, short of feed and water, constantly on the gallop, and always ready to gallop, in extremes of heat and cold, and this life lasts for very many years—not for a season or two only.

It is absurd to put against the life work of an Arab horse the life work of a thoroughbred—*e.g.*, like Sysonby, said to have been one of the greatest horses of his generation, and trained and pampered, whose aggregate of all his races after all his nursing was twelve and a half miles. A life work of twelve and a half miles to judge a horse by! To compare this with the work of an Arab horse in his own country, who often lives for over twenty years, and is from time to time ridden 100 miles, or even more at a stretch, without being dismounted, badly fed, and short of water!

I do not say that there are not some very grand thoroughbreds, where the Arab blood comes out strongly, but they are like angels' visits, few and far between, and are getting fewer and farther between every year. That necessarily follows from breeding from mongrels on both sides for such a long period and for one purpose only.

To breed in and in is not always necessarily disadvantageous with a pure breed, but with a hybrid animal the progeny can never be relied on, especially when both parents are hybrid. Even if one were pure and the other mongrel, you can never be sure when or how the offspring will throw back. And I think it may be taken that these few grand thoroughbreds, which I just referred to, are horses in which the Arab prepotency has made itself felt and in which the Arab blood has predominated. Where that is the case, you may get a

THE THOROUGHBRED

fairly good horse. Where the blood of the cocktail on the great heavy horse predominates, you get weeds.

Even in the progeny of the exceptionally excellent ones, in which the Arab blood has predominated, there is a tendency more or less to reversion, and the progeny cannot be absolutely or always relied upon. You cannot rely on their breeding true. As the *Times* observed on December 15, 1905 : " Biologists tell us that the more decidedly specialized an animal is, the less fit he is to cope with change or fit himself to new environment."

Now the thoroughbred is highly specialized to sprint, and, if he do that well a few times in his life, his work is done.

Without Arab blood there could have been no thoroughbred, for all his good qualities are derived from his Arab blood, while his softness and tricks and want of stamina come from his baser ancestors. He was a great success so long as the Arab was used, but, since the Arab has been abandoned, the thoroughbred has become a failure. What can you expect when you breed from sires and dams both of mixed blood without reinvigorating it— " nondescript, ill-bred, scrubby sires " ? which is a desscription used by an expert in Victoria.

Since my former book appeared, matters have got worse, and a continuance in the same line of breeding for another fifty years would make the thoroughbred perfectly useless for all purposes, except as a gambling machine, and it is doubtful if he would be fit even for that. The *Field* recently stated that " if the thoroughbred inbreeding continues on the same lines for much longer there will probably be a collapse of the English thoroughbred."

Coming from such a journal, that is amazing corroboration of my views. If it had been a parson who had said so, the " sports " might have sneered, but they scarcely can do so at the utterances of one of the most respected authorities in the world. If they should do so, " the man in the street " and the farmers, whom I principally address, will surely have common sense enough to judge fairly between a " sport " and an able and honourable editor. A " sport " is very seldom if ever a " sportsman."

As things are, the noblest animal in creation is bred nominally to furnish innocent amusement for good Christian men, but practically to put money into the pockets of the rooks—gentlemen designated by Mr. Frank T. Bullen in his latest work as " dirty-handed filchers of other men's earnings." The matter is of supreme importance ; and I shall have to touch upon this branch of the subject again.

That I do the thoroughbred no injustice is proved by numerous articles and criticisms in the press during the last few years, which should be a lesson to all honest men. I shall presently give some extracts, mostly without comment, because they speak for themselves, and I shall give the extracts from the *Times* a chapter to themselves. I give the dates, so that readers can verify the extracts and obtain the benefit of any qualifying observations if any such appear. I think none will be found. My contention is that no amount of excellence in six or eight or ten great stallions can get rid of the fact that for the most part the breed is now a failure.

In my former book I had the advantage of being able to quote a great Australian Governor, and, before giving the quotations from the *Times*, I will quote even a greater Governor of a more recent date, from the *Australasian* of November 6, 1909, where the Governor-General, Lord Dudley, said that at all the shows he had visited throughout Australia he had been disappointed with the hacks. There was, he thought, deterioration, and, to

THE THOROUGHBRED

ascertain if that were so, he had caused a letter to be written to the Indian Government asking if the type of Australian horse purchased for remounts was on the decline. The answer was to the effect that, while those received were satisfactory, the stamp of horse required for officers' chargers and for the artilllery was hard to procure.

Lord Dudley had possibly noticed the " touchiness " of some of his Australian racing friends about their horses, which was possibly the reason why he applied to India to justify his opinion as to the deterioration of Australian horses; but whether that was or was not his reason, the reply to his application to India fully supported what he said. And, although I feel great regret at such a terrible failure of my country's horseflesh, it is a satisfaction to me to be able to quote the authority of the Earl of Dudley in support of views which I have propounded, but for expressing which I have been sharply attacked. I ought rather to receive credit.

CHAPTER XV

DETERIORATION, AS GATHERED FROM THE *TIMES*

WITH the view of ascertaining whether the opinion that hybrids are not to be relied upon to breed true is supportable, I watched the *Times* for the last year or two so as to discover if it contained any guidance on the matter. It seems to me that the information to be gathered there is alarmingly suggestive, and goes to prove not only that these hybrids cannot be depended upon to breed true, but almost to demonstrate the " passing of the thoroughbred." Various opinions from that paper, for the most part appearing in the sporting intelligence columns, as to racing, follow.

No one that I can find has ever ventured to say that the true Arab is soft, and but very few have ventured to call him roguish. I believe that in most cases where they have so spoken of an Arab they have referred to a horse which was not a pure Arab, for there are Afghan Arabs, Beluchee Arabs, Syrian Arabs, Persian Arabs, Arabs and Arabs of the towns, and half-caste Arabs of all sorts, not even " sons of horses " in the real Arab sense. Beluchees, Afghans, Syrians, Persians, and all these Eastern races can lie about horses nearly as well as a Christian, but, as Lady Anne Blunt says in one of her books, although a Bedouin Arab of the desert can lie unblushingly in a general way, you may rely on it that he will never lie about his pure-bred horse. It is his religion, and he is in honour bound to speak the truth about his horse.

There are also Australian Arabs, some of which have, perhaps, a little more Arab blood in them than a mule, but it is really shocking to see some of the ponies that pass as Arabs in Australia. Of course, there are some pure breds, but as a rule the owners of these do not let it be sufficiently known that they are pure, and take no steps to expose the pretences of the hybrids. Thus the Arab gets blamed as throwing indifferent stock.

Quotations from the *Times* :

May 31, 1900.—" In England they no longer keep horses for the business of their daily lives, but for racing and hunting, on which the ideas of the majority are founded."

June 10, 1907.—" Stayers in the top class for speed are few and far between, and their number would appear to be rapidly decreasing. . . . Only a small proportion are able to win over a course of a mile and a half, and only an odd one could get beyond that distance. . . . The fair stayer should be the rule and the sprinter the exception, whereas it is now the other way about, and matters are going from bad to worse. . . . A curtailment of the sprinting, and a little more sense on the part of breeders is wanted. . . . The style of modern breeding tends to the reproduction of size and speed, and if stamina come in, it is a mere matter of chance."

June 10, 1907.—" What is the use of breeding horses of commanding size, great quality, and bone and substance, which please the eye, if there is no stamina to back up these outward virtues ?"

It then complains of the necessity for using blinkers in so many cases.

July 1, 1907.—" Last week's racing was more conspicuous for quantity than quality."

July 29, 1907.—" The Goodwood fields were very large indeed, but a huge majority of the runners were platers only;" and the *Times* denounced the softness and roguishness which are so frequently to be found in the modern race-horse.

August 26, 1907.—" The failure of the modern thoroughbred to stand continuous training is becoming a very serious matter. Slieve Gallion's Derby defeat was due to lack of stamina. . . . Beyond all doubt a greater number of sound stallions than there are is necessary."

September 6, 1907.—" The cast racer is generally a weed, the hunter wants both bone and substance, the coach-horse has decayed, and the Norfolk cob is not what he was."

September 8, 1904.—" At the sale of yearlings at Doncaster, a great many lots were sent back or disposed of for nominal prices."

December 5, 1904.—" The painful lack of reputable material is usually associated with melancholy entertainments which are calculated to bring contempt and discredit upon the sport."

July 17, 1906.—" The number of useless malformed and unhealthy horses has increased disproportionately to the increase of healthy animals, and the state of things at the present time is almost of a dangerous character."

August 3, 1906.—" The whole field (at Goodwood) compared very unfavourably so far as quality is concerned, with most of the previous winners of this coveted trophy, and never, perhaps, has the field been so poor as it was yesterday."

March 18, 1907.—" We are entirely without cup horses of high class. The Grand National has rather collapsed lately owing to the many scratchings which have taken place, and to the fact that several of those still left in are more or less under suspicion. Thus, Ascetics Silver has a bad habit of breaking bloodvessels. Wolf's Folly

May 14, 1907.—" The showyard sets the standard type, and there is no denying that there is scarcely a breed of long standing which has not at one time or another suffered some injury from imprudence in humouring fancy or fashion, and it is a tedious and expensive business to restore valuable characteristics which have been sacrificed in this way."

May 20, 1907.—" Amphion, though a brilliant horse, was—as are most of his stock—best at a mile or a little beyond. Some of the best-looking Gallinules have been sprinters only."

May 27, 1907.—" Baltinglass played a poor part, and the winner was a cast-off from Lord Carnarvon's stables. The Hurst Park Mile was too far for Freeborn, who may now be considered a third-rater only. The two-year-olds which ran at Hurst Park were moderate. All Black probably failed because he could not get the distance. Anyhow, he must now be set down as an imposter."

Ibid.—" The stock of this great horse [Isinglass] are dead out of luck at present, and have not won a single race so far as the season has gone."

June 3, 1907.—" Newmarket opinions of Galvani vary very greatly, some of the accounts being full of praise while others are to the effect that he tires at the end of a long gallop, and that he cannot get much further than a mile and a quarter."

(This is an indication of the uncertain conduct of the thoroughbred, and how little he is really understood.)

June 10, 1907.—" The most disappointing feature of the Derby is the dearth of stayers. Stayers in the top class for speed are few and far between, and their number would appear to be rapidly decreasing. Big, handsome and grand-looking colts are found in every annual crop of three-year-olds, but only a small proportion are able to win over a course of a mile and a half."

June 27, 1907.—" It is a curious fact that, although the Arab cannot compete with a Waler on the racecourse, he quite holds his own on a hard polo ground. The truth is that Britons (being a nation of shopkeepers, motorists, and what not) for some reason consider themselves a nation of horsemen, and think that they have nothing to learn. Consequently, their methods of training chargers, hunters, or polo ponies are too often casual, and the results fall far below what Frenchmen, Germans, or Italians can obtain. Let our polo players, therefore, in common with the rest of the nation, 'wake up' from their self-complacent slumber."

July 20, 1907.—" His Majesty won the Eclipse Stakes with Diamond Jubilee seven years ago. Winners have since, with the exception of Ard Patrick, been of moderate class, and it can hardly be said that yesterday's field was of much account. There was, in point of fact, a lack of winning classic form among the runners. There was no winner of the Derby, St. Leger, or any other classic race included in the seven who did duty, and there was no cup horse of high class. The field was, indeed, composed of two or three who were just useful and no more, and of two or three who had no pretensions to be running for such a race. Lally's defeat suggested that a mile and a quarter was further than he cared to travel. The others were not seriously considered."

July 29, 1907.—" Fields [at Liverpool, etc.] were very large indeed, but a huge majority of runners were platers only. Amongst the runners was the Derby winner Orby, who, in the valuable Atlantic Stakes, gave a truly wretched performance. It is, by the way, worthy of note that much of the softness and roguishness which is so frequently to be found in the modern race-horse is attributed to excessive inbreeding."

August 13, 1907.—" As for the quality of sires shown at the twentieth show of thoroughbreds, there is no need for any great amount of praise; some good horses were there, and many passable ones, but there was a marked lightness of limb in many of the exhibits, and quality has been better in former years."

August 26, 1907.—" That the Derby winner should have collapsed is a matter of general regret, but the failure of the modern thoroughbred to stand continued training is becoming a very serious matter. Spearmint was unable to compete, and in the previous year Cicero failed to stand training during the late summer, and, although he ran again as a four-year-old, he was not really of much account. Indeed, he ran only twice in his third season, beating a solitary opponent, Shilfa, at Newmarket in the spring, and running like a very moderate horse in the Ascot Cup. Little more than a fortnight hence the last classic race of the year will be decided, and the lot left in are not likely to do much towards upholding the prestige of the race. Slieve Gallion's defeat was due to lack of stamina, and he has the cut and general style of a first-rate miler rather than a horse who can win over a distance of ground."

October 21, 1907.—" Colonel Hall Walker's colt went to pieces, and so far has not recovered his form. Galvani went to pieces last spring."

November 11, 1907.—" The Sefton Steeplechase was practically a fiasco, for of the fifteen runners ten came to grief, and only five completed the race. The Liverpool Autumn Cup was almost as big a fiasco as the steeplechase, for the race was easily won by Menu, a despised outsider."

November 25, 1907.—" The Manchester November Handicap was not a great success. The twenty runners, which were anticipated a week ago, dwindled down to half that number, and there was an absence of class amongst the runners. They were a poorish lot."

December 25, 1907.—" The flat racing season of 1907 has not been in any respect a brilliant one. Certain horses have, as a matter of course, distinguished themselves, but their performances are only good by comparison. The fillies which were the winners of the Oaks and the 1,000 Guineas are in all probability about a stone and a half behind the average three-year-old filly. The 2,000 winner, Slieve Gallion, in the Derby was thoroughly pumped out soon after the straight was reached, and ran home a swerving well-beaten horse. And the three-year-olds, with the exception of Wool Winder and Galvani, are made to look very moderate indeed."

January 1, 1908.—" Outside the group of people who are interested in horse-breeding, very little is known as to the exact state of affairs which prevails. It may not even be generally known that the horse-breeding industry is in danger. In hunter breeding there are many disappointments for every success."

January 2, 1908.—" It is certainly the case on the Turf that the present group of riders are like the horses they are riding, a very moderate lot."

February 21, 1908.—" A very large proportion of the horses foaled are only fit to work on the farm."

It was stated further that there was a growing tendency to breed show horses, for the horse that fetched the most money was generally the horse with the most action, and not the most useful animal. Lieutenant-General Sir John Frazer was cited, who fully agreed with what Sir E. Hutton had said as to Australia : that horse-breeding in Australia had deteriorated to a very great extent. Mr. Algernon Turnor, Chairman of the Brood Mare Society, affirmed that the general utility horse was an animal, as a rule, the result of haphazard and chance. We had not bred him on any sound system or scientific lines, and the result was that we bred a large proportion of misfits.

March 3, 1908.—" As the chosen sires are ex-race-horses or horses which have been bred for racing, but owing to accident have not run, it follows that only second-raters are sent up for competition."

March 11, 1908.—" There were runners enough [at Lincoln and Liverpool] in all conscience, but it was a case of quantity rather than equality, and it is quite probable that the big handicap was never contested by a poorer lot of horses. It must be admitted that there was no horse of anything approaching high class in the field."

May 8, 1908.—" The twenty-two runners for the two-year-old plate at Newmarket were apparently a poor lot."

May 11, 1908.—" Only brief comment is necessary about the sport [at Hurst Park]. For the most part the competitors were of comparatively small account."

May 21, 1908.—" It is impossible to avoid the conclusion that the three-year-olds are extremely bad this season."

May 23, 1908.—" To all present appearances, none of the horses engaged in the day's sport [Newmarket] can be worth more than the merest passing comment."

June 12, 1908.—" The Manchester Cup, worth £3,000, has been won by good horses. There seems to be nothing to rank with these in the present entry; it must presumably be a very moderate field of horses in which Baltinglass is set to carry 8 stone 10 pounds."

June 20, 1908.—" Ascot on the last day was so far true to its traditions that few things happened, the occurrence of which could have been reasonably expected. Most extraordinary of all was the success of Mr. Croker's Rhodora. On Wednesday the filly ran, and the general belief was that she could scarcely be beaten. So bad was her performance then that it really seemed useless to send her again, but to-day she won easily, a strongly marked contrast to her hopeless failure a couple of days previously."

June 22, 1908.—" Several English officers took part in this competition [at the International Show], and were badly beaten by Belgians and others. It seemed to be that the horses were in fault rather than the riders. Many of the animals were weedy, undersized, and common looking. It was plain enough that better horses, better schooled, would be required to put the home contingent on equal terms with their European neighbours."

Ibid.—" Some of the other horses which failed [at Ascot] have capacity which they will not exert. This was notably the case with Vamose. Flying Fox, when in training, was stubborn, and doubt always existed as to whether he would start. He stood still, and refused to line up with the other horses until an attendant picked some grass and coaxed him back. Vamose starts but declines to exert himself; nor, indeed, it is to be feared, did His Majesty's ' Perrier ' give a very generous exhibition. Mr. Leopold Rothschild's Radium is another horse with a disinclination to run his races out; and, to come to an animal of less importance, Weathercock simply remained and put back his ears. The hoods he and so many others wear are not put on without good reason. There appears to be an unfortunate increase of cowardice or wilfulness among the horses of to-day. Strickland has won his last four races without having beaten anything that can be accepted as good. Captain Greer's Gallivant struck some observers, including his owner, as having given an ungenerous display, and no great hopes were entertained of His Majesty's Oakmere, who ran second. The Windsor Castle Stakes must be set down as a fiasco, and the three who had been thought far the best were really never in the race."

June 27, 1908.—" It takes some time to establish a horse's character. The consequence is that the owners of geese sometimes find it hard to persuade themselves that they are not possessed of swans. There is not the slightest doubt that Dalgety is a very bad colt. No good reason exists for supposing that Mr. Raphael's St. Wolf is anything like a good one. The New Strand Handicap brought out some horses of which it had once been hoped that they would make distinguished names for themselves, till the disagreeable truth was put beyond doubt that a five-furlong course was about as far as they could gallop at top speed."

June 29, 1908.—" Really good horses are exceedingly rare; an owner seldom finds himself in possession of one. Some owners are never so fortunate as to do so, after

DETERIORATION, FROM THE *TIMES*

many years devoted to the production of thoroughbred stock. Not a few of the leading owners have passed long lives in futile attempts to win ' classic ' races."

July 2, 1908.—" The racing [Newmarket] was distinctly moderate in quality. Linacre was regarded at having the best chance in the Duke of Cambridge's Handicap, if only he could be induced to start. For a long time he evinced the strongest indisposition to start at all, or even to stand with his head in the right direction."

July 3, 1908.—" Cargill cantered to the post as if he were reluctant to stretch himself. The fears expressed that Madame de Lubise might prove to be lacking in speed were justified. She looked well, but could not go the pace when an effort was required. It was a field of moderate horses to contest so rich a prize as £6,000."

July 4, 1908.—" The Sceptre filly never looked likely to win. She ran sideways all the time. His Majesty's Oakmere came out in the Princess Plate [Newmarket] wearing blinkers, the too familiar indication of something defective in temper or courage. It was stated, indeed, that his poor display at Sandown last week was attributable to the fact that he had seized hold of another horse's tail in the course of the race, and devoted his energies to gnawing this instead of galloping."

July 6, 1908.—" Much of the racing at Newmarket First July meeting was of a very moderate description. Of the three supposed best horses in training, White Knight is the only one who has sustained his reputation. In the Hurstbourne Stakes for the two-year-olds this year nothing of mark is entered. The best is probably Valens. He seems to have little to beat. At Pontefract, competitors are for the most part of modest ability."

(*Date mislaid.*)—" The Royal Commission on Horse-breeding in their eleventh Report state that there is a demand for a greater number of sound stallions than there are; as to the truth of which remark there can be no question, and the remarks of the Commission referring to the future are of a pessimistic character."

July 8, 1908.—" In the autumn of 1906 Mr. W. Clark gave 1,000 guineas for Rambling Rector, who, as a two-year-old, was a failure. He is an example of what very bad bargains can be made."

July 9, 1908.—" The three-year-olds started in the race [Bibury Club Meeting] were of very small account, with the exception, perhaps, of Gyges, and though he was certainly third to St. Wolf for the Sandringham Foal Stakes, he carried a very low weight."

July 15, 1908.—" There was little disappointment [at Newmarket], as not much had been expected. Even Radium's owner does not entertain the idea that he is usually inclined to struggle when the moment arrives for special exertion. Bushranger is an unmistakable rogue."

July 18, 1908.—" Lord Rosebery recognized the hopelessness of sending Olympus to oppose good horses, or, if this be not an accurate description of the Eclipse Stakes field, the phrase may be amended; for to speak of the animals which took part in this race as good would, it is feared, be incorrect. It must be concluded that the handsome little daughter of St. Frusquin and Glare does not stay, for she faded out of the race before she was half-way up the hill. On several occasions luck has decided the issue, for the stake has been won by other than the best animals. White Eagle, however, does not stay a mile and a quarter, even in a slow-run race. All the runners were moderate animals."

July 20, 1908.—" The three-year-olds before the Derby were denounced as bad. Their performances are full of contradictions, and, as a general rule, when horses of the same age constantly beat each other ' running in and out,' it is nearly always found that they are bad as a class. White Eagle and Lesbia are so little able to stay that they can have no sort of chance for the St. Leger."

July 22, 1908.—" Noctuiform has at length won a race [Leicester]. In 1906 he won nothing. Last year he ran seven times without even making his way into the first three, and the £100 Badgate Park Plate is the only return his owner has had for an expenditure of several thousands. He has hitherto declined to exert himself, but in this race his opponents were so poor that no exertion could have been necessary."

August, 1908.—" There are very few horses who run brilliantly, if the phrase may be allowed, over short courses, and who also maintain their speed over a distance of ground, or perhaps it should be said have a reserve of speed to draw upon after a long course has been covered. The Jockey Club Cup at Newmarket was such a burlesque that, after the starter had despatched a small field and leisurely mounted his pony to canter back, he actually overtook the horses who were supposed to be racing. The best of the moderate opponents of Madame de Loubise seems to be Lord Rosebery's Benzonian, who was never more than a second-class colt, and Lord Howard de Walden's Cargill—an animal not calculated to inspire enthusiasm. It is, of course, unfortunate that so much money—a sum which might have produced several excellent races—should be allotted to such poor animals."

Ibid.—" Buckwheat made a comparatively poor show. Blankney II. for a few seconds looked a possible victor, but he could not sustain his effort. Of the six saddled for the Cup, only three were really to be regarded as serious competitors."

August 1, 1908.—" The Nassau Stakes [Goodwood] for three-year-old fillies closed with sixty-four entries, only a couple of whom found their way to the post. Inability to stay the mile and a half explained the absence of many. French Partridge and several others who are in training have shown speed over short courses, but are of little use in good company at a mile."

August 10, 1908.—" At intervals, an Ormonde, a St. Simon, an Isinglass, a Persimmon, a Flying Fox appears, but animals of really the highest class come only at intervals, and in ordinary years those that stand out at all constitute so small a percentage that in the nature of things they can be seldom seen. A great many races took place last week, but probably no horse that can properly be described as good was saddled, and not many that can be held to approach goodness. Though the King's filly Marie Legraye won her race at Brighton, there is no reason to suppose that she is anything like a good animal. If His Majesty's other filly could only be trusted to do her best there might be something of a career before her, but there is no denying that the breed is shifty."

August 18, 1908.—" Mr. Buchanan's Noctuiform was apparently provided with a race [Windsor] in which he had nothing to do. There were only two other runners of most modest pretensions, but Noctuiform would not gallop, and finished last; and the truth can no longer be disguised that he is useless for racing purposes, and this is the more unfortunate, as he may transmit his character to his offspring when sent to the stud."

August 21, 1908.—" Last year Galore was rated a little more than a stone behind the best of the two-year-olds, but she has deteriorated and does not stay. Jack Horner made his seventh appearance [Stockton]. Mesmer won the Elton Maiden Plate; it is not often that so poor a colt secures so good a stake."

August 24, 1908.—" It is useless to regret that Parole had not worthier antagonists in the Hardwicke Stakes. Racing is likely to be below the average to-morrow and on the following two days, as some of the most famous events can only bring out poor fields. It is unfortunate that this week the races mentioned can hardly sustain their reputation."

August 25, 1908.—" Perseverance II., judged from a Newmarket standpoint, is a very bad animal in spite of her parentage, Persimmon—Reminiscence."

August 28, 1908.—" That Blankney II. should have won the Gimcrack Stakes [York] says little for the opposition. Since Newmarket he has been out on four occasions without in any way distinguishing himself."

DETERIORATION, FROM THE *TIMES*

August 29, 1908.—" Moderate sport took place [Gatwick]. No good horse was seen. It is hard to say what sort of horses are so bad that it is not worth while to keep them in training. Fruitful is a mare with a rooted disinclination to race, and College evinced no anxiety to do so."

September 1, 1908.—" His Majesty's Cynosure ran very badly at Brighton a month ago, his one outing this year. He also ran once rather ignominously last season, and is quite unworthy to carry the Royal colours. The best of the animals engaged [at Derby] are of no more than the very moderate description, an unsuccessful selling plater being in the handicap rather nearer to the top than to the bottom."

September 2, 1908.—" Noctuiform either could not or would not gallop [Derby], and he must be set down as quite worthless for racing. The style in which Weltonia cantered home for the Ascot Cup seemed to proclaim him to be something better than a good horse, but he has been a failure at the stud."

September 7, 1908.—" There is an idea that Radium is not entirely to be trusted. White Eagle's prospects do not seem so good after his failure at Derby, while there was always a grave doubt as to whether he would last over the St. Leger course. International is, it is to be feared, a confirmed rogue."

September 10, 1908.—" Horses who could win, if they would, unfortunately appear to be growing more numerous. Mr. Buchanan has a notorious one in Noctuiform, and his Temeraire seems to be another."

September 24, 1908.—" Vamose is an altogether unworthy brother of Flying Fox. St. Cyril's jockey began to flourish his whip in a manner no doubt disconcerting to a colt of what it may be complimentary to call an uncertain disposition. A bad wind infirmity rendered it necessary to put a tube in his throat, and he has much deteriorated. It is a little melancholy to find in humble £100 stakes horses who have at one time seemed capable of making great names for themselves."

September 28, 1908.—" Seven-and-twenty horses went to the post for the Whatcombe Handicap. Mr. E. A. Wigan's four-year-old proved good enough to win, which, considering his antecedents, does not say much for those whom he beat."

September 30, 1908.—" Aboyne is a very bad animal. A quiet day of sport [Newmarket] was relieved from insignificance by the running of Bayardo in the Buckenham Stakes."

October 2, 1908.—" The daughter of Cyllene and Sceptre has a higher reputation than she deserved. Her inferiority to Mr. Fairie's Bayardo is hardly to be estimated, but she did not seem to have much to beat in the Triennial Stakes. The Sceptre filly is never likely to enhance the fame of her dam. Than Illustrious there is no greater jade in training."

October 8, 1908.—" The sport generally [Leicester] was of an extremely moderate description, but the son of St. Simon and Laodamia earned a character for shiftiness of disposition, it is to be feared with reason. Kilcarby has won a couple of races, but from poor opponents, and can only be set down as a disappointment."

October 13, 1908.—" The Newmarket Oaks closed in October, 1906, since which time it has been demonstrated that many of the fillies concerned in it do not stay."

October 14, 1908.—" This handsome daughter of Ayrshire and Maid of the Mint is such a nervous, excitable creature that it is desirable to relieve her from the stress of work, more of which would be likely to impair her functions as a brood mare, and the blood is of the highest value."

October 17, 1908.—" The mare decidedly forced Bayardo to gallop, which he did with his mouth open and his ears back, usually symptoms either of distress or of ungenerous disposition. Royal Realm, it is to be feared, has no heart for a fight. The son of Persimmon and Sandblast has been out eight times, and this was his eighth failure."

November 20, 1908.—" A number of hard-working animals figure in the Stayers Handicap [Gatwick], that is to say, hard-worked considering what is usually required from a race-horse; indeed, the thoroughbred in training has for the most part a luxurious time."

October 21, 1908.—" The meeting [Nottingham] has sunk to humble dimensions and the chief prize to-day is the Midland Nursery of £300, the class in which is not high. The average value of the animals that will run is very small. . . . The number of bad horses who appear on race-courses especially at this time of the season is remarkable. Not a few of the starters run so wretchedly that it seems impossible they can win any sort of stake. During the afternoon [Gatwick] eighty-eight horses were saddled, and if the average value could be ascertained it would come out at a very low figure. Cuffs showed the disinclination to gallop which is characteristic of him. It is to be feared that roguishness in horses is becoming more and more common. The fact, indeed, is confessed, though no remedy seems to be suggested."

October 22, 1908.—" Punctilio has fallen off in a fashion characteristic of so many young horses who begin the season successfully."

November 16, 1908.—" In speculations as to what horse will win, the only thing certain is that deductions will far more frequently prove wrong than right."

November 18, 1908.—" Strange things happen, and not the least strange is that so poor a creature as Li Hung, even with the weight of 6 stone 4 pounds contemptuously allotted to him, should have contrived to win. It could not have been expected that a race of this comparative importance would fall to so inferior an animal. Bombastas' winning affords proof of the exceedingly feeble nature of his opponents."

November 23, 1908.—" Hurdle racing and steeplechasing are a variety of the sport which, in the words of the late Lord Suffolk, ' constituted the recognized refuge of all outcasts human and equine from the legitimate Turf.' Every man did what seemed good to him, and in many cases this seemed very bad indeed. All the horses of whom most was expected, when the season began, have repeatedly failed. Prospector did so from infirmity, as did St. Cyril. Lesbia was withdrawn. White Eagle and White Knight have lost more races than they have won. The year, so far as can be at present ascertained, has produced nothing of undoubted merit. Deceptive hopes are often raised by the way in which the young horses carry themselves. Many of them, good-looking and well-bred, soon go to pieces when put to gallop half a mile at racing pace. Roseate Dawn, since he carried off the Spring Cup, has consistently failed. Spate is given to disappointing the expectations of his friends."

November 25, 1908.—" Dinneford retires from the Turf, with a faded reputation, sadly deteriorated."

December 7, 1908.—" The Newmarket Sales will occupy the present week. As often as not the own brothers and sisters of famous animals prove useless for racing purposes, an argument which is not to be explained away. If it rarely happens thus, excuses might be found, but it is far too frequent an occurrence to be set aside as having no significance."

December 14, 1908.—" Though owners may be intent on getting rid of the worst animals, it happens on occasions that those cast off prove better than those which are kept. A considerable number have been those, the wish of whose owners to see the last of them is perfectly comprehensible. It frequently happens that mares who have been consistently unsuccessful as race-horses have been the dams of great winners, and those who have distinguished themselves by winning the chief prizes of the turf, have failed to produce anything of any value. A good many animals were sold or offered for sale simply because their owners were tired of their incapacity or indisposition to race. No fewer than 375 horses during the last flat racing season failed to get off, and were practically beaten before the race began. Experience has shown that exclusive breeding, while conducive to the preservation of type and fixed characteristics, is liable to beget constitutional weakness and impaired stamina."

January 2, 1909.—" It was found out that certain good-looking horses which had never been in training or had proved abject failures on the turf had been awarded prizes, merely because of good looks, and had signally failed with regard to their stock. Good-looking horses, which had been hopelessly incapable when sent to a trainer, or which had never been trained at all because of inability to gallop, were at times carefully kept and prepared for these premiums. The horse industry in the United Kingdom is gradually declining."

January 16, 1909.—" It is sad to observe the large number of horses who refuse to do their best."

January 25, 1909.—" A not inconsiderable proportion of young animals are found to be so obviously wanting in essential qualities that they are not put in training ; others, in the course of their preparation, show that it is hopeless to persevere with them. There are, again, those who are in one way or another, by accident or illness, incapacitated for racing, . . . for many young ones, whose action is irreproachable and who have begun to suggest great possibilities, are found to lose their action after a comparatively short distance has been covered at full speed."

February 2, 1909.—" It is considered necessary to find occupation for bad horses, which accounts for the selling hurdle race and steeplechase."

Ibid.—" Neither on the Continent of Europe nor in the great horse-breeding countries of Australia and North and South America can the excellence of the breed be maintained without constantly returning to the fountain-head for both sires and mares."

March 22, 1909.—" As a whole the horses to whom the chief events fell last season by no means compare favourably with the majority of their predecessors. At Lincoln anything approaching to a good horse was a rarity."

March 24, 1909.—" The significance of the race [Lincoln Handicap] apparently is that we have a number of particularly bad handicap horses in training."

March 26, 1909.—" As a rule, two-thirds of the starters [in the Grand National] fail to finish : falling, refusing, or being pulled up."

April 1, 1909.—" When a horse is so lightly handicapped as to make the result of a race appear almost inevitable, he is frequently beaten."

April 20, 1909.—" Only animals of moderate capacity are engaged in the Great Metropolitan Stakes. Temeraire is a horse of moods. Chat apparently can win only if the others are of very little merit."

April 22, 1909.—" As invariably happens, several of the eighteen starters of whom much was expected did every little ; that, indeed, is a matter of course. Most of the seven appear of small capacity." (Epsom.)

April 26, 1909.—" Seedcake and the others are bad animals. Bad horses are apt to beat each other, that is to say, their ' form ' is frequently not to be depended upon. Seventeen worse animals have perhaps never gone to the post to run for £1,000." (Newmarket.)

May 7, 1909.—" The race for the cup itself [Chester] was in truth of no great importance, after Yentoi had given vent to his exuberance by a few kicks. The fact that Walter Tyrrell won the Stamford Plate does not say much in favour of those he beat."

May 12, 1909.—" Of the thirty originally entered, five ran, and three of these were not seriously considered." (Newmarket.)

May 14, 1909.—" Nimrod effectually resisted Maher's endeavours to make him leave the Birdcage. After an extraordinary display of temper, the intention of starting him had to be abandoned ; he, in fact, declined to start." (Newmarket.)

May 21, 1909.—" The York Meeting ended somewhat tamely, the animals engaged not being a sort that evoke much interest."

May 29, 1909.—" Frequently owners regret the sparseness of their nominations ; very much more frequently the regret is in the opposite direction, that they have put worthless horses into a number of races for which they can have no chance."

June 7, 1909.—" Once more Rushcutter has failed to do what was thought to be well within his powers ; it was generally supposed that he would at length redeem his various failures, but it was not to be." (Manchester.)

June 14, 1909.—" Walter Tyrrell took a race at Chester. He beat an inferior field there, and is himself small and unattractive. Dandyprat was lightly weighted [at Gatwick], and the allowance proved highly serviceable. Without it he would have been beaten. This colt is rather a common place sort of animal."

Ibid.—" It is understood that on Whirlpool no dependence can be placed, and that Mr. J. B. Joel's The Story is a hopeless sort of animal in the hands of a boy. He went as far as he cared to go [at Newbury], and the efforts of his small jockey to make him go further were not of the very least avail. Smuggler, carrying only 6 stone 9 pounds, was left to win, and at the same time to show what wretchedly poor horses were running. A number of third-rate animals came out for the Kennet Two-year-old Plate."

June 16, 1909.—" There seems reason to believe that there were some animals of more than average merit in the Coventry Stakes [Ascot], a suggestion, however, which is advanced with full recollection of how frequently in former years similar ideas have turned out to be wrong."

June 18, 1909.—" Princesse de Galles' victory [at Ascot] was, nevertheless, a surprise. As so frequently happens on the Turf, the reverse of what had been expected took place. Cargill was a promising colt before he broke down, and his soundness is now probably open to question, but here he proved good enough to do what was wanted of him. In spite of swerving about the course, and so losing several lengths, Dark Ronald won with something to spare. The truth about Glasgerion doubtless is that he retains his fine speed, but cannot stay. The first event on the card was one of those races which are scarcely ever seen elsewhere than at Ascot, with only four starters, but all animals of reputation. Of the half-dozen horses saddled for the Cup, only Santa Strata and Siberia were supposed to have real prospects of success. Yentoi could not possibly win; not much seemed to be expected. Aquarelle really seemed out of place in a Cup field. Bomba ran very moderately at Epsom, and worse still previously at Newbury. His Majesty's Minoru had two indifferent colts against him in the St. James's Palace Stakes."

July 2, 1909.—" The filly proved herself a jade. Balnault did not run well, and the race went to Briolet, bought last year at a weeding-out sale. Norman III. ran badly, Galvani faltered, Your Majesty seemed to fail from inability to stay, White Eagle is not regarded as a stayer, and to have beaten him is by no means evidence that Your Majesty can last. Primer is an uncertain animal. Glasgerion looked as if he was about to win until the post was nearly reached, when he suddenly flagged." (Newmarket.)

July 28, 1909.—" Merry Jack looked as if his success were assured, but when his jockey endeavoured to send him on to win, he threw up his head and opened his mouth in a style which indicated deliberate refusal, leaving the race to the filly." (Goodwood.)

July 30, 1909.—" The Plate [Goodwood] was won by Lagos, another son of Santoi, who has run so shiftily on occasions that it can never be guessed what he may do. The son of Rock Sand and Sagacity would not exert himself, and could not be made to do so. Neil Gow won, but it was agreed that he did not do so in altogether satisfactory style. He seemed reluctant to stride out; he is a singularly lazy colt. There is a suspicion there may be something of trickiness. Five moderate horses came out in the Cup."

August 13, 1909.—" The Story, however, did manage to secure the Devonshire Plate [Kempton], but in circumstances which cannot be advanced as a proof of his ability to stay. The fact is, that a valuable stake— £1,000—was contested by bad animals."

August 23, 1909.—" There were two £500 stakes at Wolverhampton, and each of them was contested by no more than three runners. Oakmere failed because he declined to put any heart into his work. In the corresponding race on the second day the winner Floriculture also displayed the cowardice which is unfortunately found in what seems to be an increasing number of cases, but the opposition was so poor that the winner was really unable to fail. Homing Pigeon won the Wynyard Plate [Stockton], and she is no better than useful."

September 3, 1909.—" Mirador has probably been overrated in consequence of having won his last four races. In none of them has he beaten any but very bad animals. When Seraphim took the Ham Stakes, it was because her opponent Merry Jack would not try. Sister Anne did badly in Wootton's hands, the Plate falling to Holy Wind, a colt who had run wretchedly in the three stakes he had contested." (Derby.)

September 6, 1909.—" Sagamore was one of the best two-year-olds of his season; but, like so many other horses in training, he frequently refuses to do his best. The son of Ian and Tathwell is another of the rogues, and his trainer was not in the least surprised to see that Maher was unable to induce him to fight out his race." (Lewes.)

September 15, 1909.—" A crowd was attracted by the Cesarewitch, notwithstanding the fact that an excep-

tionally poor field were to assemble for the race. It
was recognized that in a collection of such indifferent
animals almost any of them might win, as the seventeen
whose numbers had been displayed began to canter to
the post."

September 20, 1909.—" The Americans won the first
match [Polo] by nine goals to six. Their ponies showed
a marked superiority. They started quicker than the
English ponies, turned inside them, and, when it came
to a stretching gallop, left them apparently without effort.
The English ponies were not so markedly inferior as in
the first match, but inferior they certainly were. The
result was a crushing defeat for England."

September 24, 1909.—" At San Sebastian, during the
past week, has been seen some of the best riding upon some
of the best horses in Europe, including two important
competitions between picked teams of officers repre-
senting the armies of seven nations. In both these events
the English team was placed last."

November 19, 1909.—" Diamond Stud was beaten for
the ninth time in ten races. If opportunities are afforded
him at the stud, it will be because of his pedigree and
appearance, not of his performances." (Derby.)

November 22, 1909.—" The possession of the winner is
not, however, a matter for much pride. The daughter
of Cyllene and Galettia is many removes from a good
animal. Mr. Fairie was not far from carrying off another
race, with a bad colt." (Derby.)

November 24, 1909.—" After vainly striving for three
years, Seedcake managed to win £100. Three of the
most forlorn animals in training constituted the opposition." (Warwick.)

December 13, 1909.—" At the Newmarket sales market,
last week, a number of mares were purchased by foreign
breeders. Of late years, England has been denuded of
much valuable blood for the purpose of founding families
on the other side of the world."

DETERIORATION, FROM THE *TIMES*

December 14, 1909.—" In to-day's programme at Nottingham, Red Cloth was considered the best of those engaged, and he is not a good animal. Calderstone is one of the six colts leased last year from their breeder by the King, but he and some of the rest have been returned as hopeless. For the rest, the fields in the hurdle races are composed of indifferent animals."

December 20, 1909.—" With every disposition to make the best of things, it cannot be pretended that the sport [at Lingfield] was more than indifferent. The steeplechase included the four most promising horses in the entry, as they had won races, and three very bad animals ran."

Ibid.—" In his fourth speech last week, Mr. Hall Walker stated there must be cordial agreement with his remarks that it would be a most unfortunate thing if the British thoroughbred lost his preponderance, not only because racing would deteriorate, but because the horse-breeding industry is one of the most important now existing in this country, and a source of employment directly and indirectly to countless numbers. When it is remembered that £40,000 has been paid for a horse—Flying Fox; that more than £50,000 has been refused for another—Bayardo; and that several other famous winners have been sold for over £30,000, what British preponderance means may be to some extent understood. In no other country have such figures ever been approached."

December 27, 1909.—" It is rather a curious fact with regard to the last four races for the Derby that six months before the races won by Spearmint, Orby, Signorinetta, and Minoru, no one for a moment took any of these names into consideration as that of a possible Derby winner."

Ibid.—" Mr. John Burns, in his speech on Christmas Day at Wandsworth Union Workhouse, said that tall men might be mated with tall women, but the progeny would not grow taller and taller, generation after generation. Either they would revert to the average, or the breed would break down somewhere."

December 29, 1909.—" The Whelp performed as if the handicapper had not been far wrong in giving him a low weight, for he tired, and dropped out a few fences from home; though he has been several times prominent in races of late, his opponents have always been of poor class."

January 6, 1910.—" The late owner of Wand gave 600 guineas for the son of Wiseman when he was a two-year-old, but was constantly disappointed at his refusal to do anything approaching to his best, and gladly got rid of him. The class of horse competing at the present time is extremely bad." (Gatwick.)

January 15, 1910.—" Napoleon knew that without good information of the enemy's strength and movements no military operation could be conducted with assurance of success. He always rode Arab horses in the field, and many of his marshals did the same, nor can anyone be surprised who has learned by experience the unequalled merits of the Arab for service in the field." (*The Military Correspondent.*)

January 17, 1910.—" At Wolverhampton only two very bad animals came out last week for the amateur riders' steeplechase."

January 24, 1910.—" Last week's sport rarely rose above a very moderate level. Whether Round Dance can last over the four miles and a half at Liverpool is a matter of pure speculation, even to his trainer. There is no reason he should not, except that so very few do."

March 9, 1910.—" Several horses whose performances were good did not please the judges, while several others who had no ' form ' to recommend them won on looks and action." (The Hunter Show.)

March 14, 1910.—" Waler ponies are more troublesome to train than Arabs or country-breds, but, when once properly broken, there is no better pony."

Ibid.—" At the polo and riding pony show at the Agricultural Hall, the Eastern sires were interesting;

and no doubt crosses of this blood are at times most desirable, for they go far towards building up the distinct breed of ponies which breeders are striving to provide."

March 15, 1910.—" Large fields—of for the most part bad horses—came out to run. Meddler, whose stock gallop fast when in the humour to do their best, which is not always; and this appears the stranger, as Meddler himself was a very generous horse."

May 6, 1910.—" Dumella created extreme disappointment. He is wayward and awkward, and never seemed to settle down to his work."

May 25, 1910.—" Horses who cannot be depended on to do anything like their best are disagreeably common; and Strickland is a notable instance: no one can guess how he may be disposed to run."

June 1, 1910.—" There were 382 entries for to-day's Derby, and a good many of the small percentage who will compete seem altogether out of place in the field."

June 15, 1910.—" The result of the Coventry Stakes [Ascot] is to suggest that there can be little to choose between a number of the younger generation, as likewise that all so far are moderate. . . . Shikaree is a bad horse, although own brother to a good one."

June 18, 1910.—" Admiral Hawke does not stay the mile and a half. Santa Fina is not to be trusted. Bomba, winner of the Cup last year, started for this minor stake, but ran as from all his races, with the exception of the Cup, he might have been expected to do. . . . Whisk Broom had seemed to show in the Trial Stakes that a mile was quite as far as he could gallop." (Ascot.)

June 20, 1910.—Horses with the exceptional speed of Bachelor's Double, which he displayed over the mile on Wednesday, are rarely found to stay." (Ascot.)

June 23, 1910.—" This race certainly seems to confirm the impression which we have previously stated, to the effect that the two-year-olds seen up to the end of the Ascot Meeting are a moderate lot." (Newbury.)

June 29, 1910.—" Romeo behaved excitedly in the paddock. A well-behaved stable companion was sent from Weyhill to soothe him by his familiar presence; but this other sadly belied his character, and set a particularly bad example, which Romeo readily followed. . . . The winner is called a nice colt, but he does not appear to help materially in the search for a really good two-year-old." (Newmarket.)

June 30, 1910.—" Yesterday we referred to the undeniable fact that Perrier inclined to run shiftily; but for once he was inclined to gallop, and, having an easy task with the light weight, he won without difficulty." (Newmarket.)

July 2, 1910.—" Sunbright refused to gallop; in fact, he made a determined attempt to bolt out of the course." (Newmarket.)

July 4, 1910.—" The existing impression that no really good young horse has been seen received confirmation."

July 11, 1910.—" Mary Carmichael was beaten, and there is no excuse to be made for her. She stopped, either because she could not last the five furlongs, or because she had no heart to try. Neil Gow has a curious temper. For the richest two-year-old race of the season there were originally 275 entries; if a dozen of them start, the event will be accepted as sufficiently successful. . . . The progeny of Laodamia, who had a great name in her day, have done little, and are as a rule faint-hearted and cowardly."

July 16, 1910.—Placidus was the only other one in the field who seemed to be worth consideration, and his unrest, not to say fractiousness, in the paddock told against him." (Sandown.)

July 14, 1910.—" There has always been a doubt as to the gameness of Decision, who more than once as a two-year-old failed to do what was believed to be well within his powers. . . . Cattaro has become hopelessly ungenerous." (Newmarket.)

July 9, 1910.—" As had seemed probable, Prester Jack did not stay the mile in the Lingfield Park Stakes."

July 18, 1910.—" Few winners of the Ascot Gold Cup reappear, and in not a few cases the reason of their withdrawal is that they are unable to run afterwards."

July 25, 1910.—" Reflection does not increase admiration for Neil Gow or Lemberg. The fear is that neither really stays. . . . Placidus is not to be trusted."

July 29, 1910.—" Bayardo was in a sulky temper [at Goodwood]. He showed reluctance to leave the paddock, and furthermore declined to join in the parade with the two who opposed him, a trick which Bayardo has played more than once."

August 15, 1910.—" King Edward, in years past, had frequently sent up particularly good-looking and, as a matter of course, notably well-bred yearlings who entirely belied their promise . . . Experience shows, however, that two-year-olds very seldom merit the description of ' good ' when, as has been constantly happening this season, they beat each other, and keep on winning by heads."

August 20, 1910.—" Of the forty entries for the Stakes [Hurst] three went to the post. . . . Louvegny has been accustomed to run over five, or rarely six, furlongs, and it is doubted whether he could last a mile, the poverty of the opposition enabling him here to do so."

August 22, 1910.—" Among the large number of Persimmon colts, bred at Sandringham, there have been none good enough to have made his retention as a sire even worth serious consideration. . . . White Eagle does not justify the belief that he was anything like a really good horse. Cheers was a coarse, clumsy animal. Jenny filly was the only animal of any approach to class who ran at Wolverhampton. . . . Spiteful filly, who carried off the Hardwicke Stakes, does not seem to be of much account. . . . Calluna gave weight to all the others in the Stockton Handicap Plate, but she cannot be magnified into anything like a good filly."

August 24, 1910.—" St. Victrix has a determined will of his own. A few days since he stood stubbornly refusing to move, and was taken home."

August, 25, 1910.—Claretoi ran wretchedly for the Bibury Cup after feeble displays at Alexandra Park and Newbury. Even as a six-year-old with 6 stone 10 pounds he appeared hopeless."

August 30, 1910.—" Strangest of all was the failure of Piedmont [at Bath], who had only one opponent, a bad filly, not long since bought out of a selling race."

September 9, 1910.—" The deficiency [at Doncaster] was the absence of high-class horses. There is never much hope of a numerous entry for a long race in which it is known that only a good horse is likely to have a chance, good horses being, indeed, always scarce."

September 12, 1910.—" Bronzino last year ran nine times, and could win nothing—he was never even second. Experience shows that the young animals who cost most frequently fail to win races."

September 22, 1910.—" Dibs was induced to start [at Windsor], which he would not do at Chester, Ascot, or Doncaster."

September 30, 1910.—" Of the 212 original entries [for the Jockey Club Stakes] only nine were produced, and the owners of most of them were embarking on an utterly hopeless enterprise."

October 21, 1910.—" Munita has done little worthy of her breeding ; she is a daughter of St. Simon and Little Eva. Brancepeth is also attractively bred ; he had never run before [Sandown Park], nor, indeed, can he be said to have done so now, for he got rid of his jockey as the starting gate flew up, and took no part in the race."

October 31, 1910.—" There is reason to fear that the three-year-olds are below the average. An excuse is made for Whisk Broom on the ground that Christmas Daisy started off at a pace which demoralized the others ;

DETERIORATION, FROM THE *TIMES*

but good horses ought not to be thus demoralized. It is on their speed that their reputations rest, and, if they cannot show it in emergencies, their claim to goodness ceases to be apparent. The experiences of the Houghton Meeting do not tend to raise the character of the three-year-olds as a class."

November 11, 1910.—" For some seasons past, inferior horses have been able to win the Liverpool Autumn Cup. A glance at the names of others who are likely to start suggests something to the detriment of each."

January 25, 1911.—" As has happened so frequently of late, nothing turned out [at Manchester] according to what seemed reasonable calculation. Why the judgment of experts should be so continually incorrect just now cannot be guessed; but so it is."

March 25, 1911.—" Thirty names appeared on the card [for the Grand National], twenty-seven of which were 'coloured' ... After walking past, the twenty-six turned round and cantered as if in an ordinary flat race, certainly creating an impression that there was no traceable decadence; although what speedily followed was unfortunately to raise doubts. ... The exhibition was far from creditable to English horsemanship—and to French horsemanship—when, after one round of the course had been completed, actually no more than five of the twenty-six remained which went on their way at a greatly diminished pace. ... To what the downfall of so many was due—how the blame should be apportioned between horses, trainers, and jockeys—is not to be hastily decided. But it assuredly cannot be said that the Grand National of 1911 was creditable to the majority of those concerned in it."

CHAPTER XVI

DETERIORATION, AS GATHERED FROM THE *AUSTRALASIAN*

ALL the extracts in this chapter are from the *Australasian* or the *Argus*, mostly the *Australasian*, which is one of the principal Australian weeklies. It is probably more widely read throughout Australia than any other weekly newspaper, and is of great weight. The extracts for the most part are from articles by sporting writers. It must be mentioned that extracts set forth here are often not continuous, and that some of them are from English correspondents referring to English horses.

November 26, 1904.—" The last dozen years, the extremely mixed animals that are exhibited in the pony classes are mostly low set horses, as unlike ponies as they could be. Such animals are weedy horses and not ponies, though they may stand under 14 hands. The true pony is a distinct race."

January 28, 1905 (quoting the *Field* as regards three-year-olds).—" During the last seven to ten years there were only six horses that could be considered really great, viz., Pretty Polly, Ard Patrick, Sceptre, Flying Fox, Persimmon, and St. Frusquin. And in Australia we hear the same story—there is a tendency to sacrifice everything to speed; the proportion of fairly good horses used to be better relatively (say fifty years ago) than now. The English thoroughbred of to-day is very fast, but he does not last long, and a great many are cursed with vile tempers. Novellina is very wayward, her sister Carrageen was not much good, and her brother Haut Novo seems useless. Taking the season 1904, the English horses are more fractious than ours. It is the exception to see a good-legged English horse of any sort, and a large number are whistlers and roarers. Many of the hunters and some of the race-horses have tubes in their throats."

March 24, 1906.—" There was a good deal of racing going on last week. The horses running were not first class. Perhaps, take them all round, the horses running at Coolgardie seem to have been a poor lot."

Ibid.—" At the Goldfields Meetings at Coolgardie weak fields and badly-conducted sport were the order of the whole meeting."

March 31, 1906.—" In Adelaide racing there is a marked absence of good horses. The last interstate list is by no means a strong one, either in the Goodwood Handicap or Adelaide Cup. A large proportion of the local horses down for handicapping have no claims for inclusion in races of this kind. When we had suburban pony racing before, the pony men proved nearly as tricky as the trotting fraternity. That ill-mannered brute Brian Boru caused a ten minutes' delay at the post, Yum-Yum was not considered, and Grey Seaton is such a thief that he could only be backed on the off-chance."

May 12, 1906.—" The Bayonet is fast, but he is a very poor stayer; he always runs with his head in the air."

June 9, 1906.—" The horses running in Adelaide now are, taken all round, a poor lot."

July 7, 1906.—" Oblivion was not the only disappointment. The National Hurdle race winner in 1904 has not in recent years run up to anything like form. Sarasati's whole career suggests that he is a sour sort of horse that will only do his best occasionally. The Sun is a very lazy horse."

August 18, 1906.—" Madden, an English jockey, was badly worried by a horse called Marigold. Fred Archer had a similar experience. Muley Edris seized him by the arm, and it was some time before the great jockey rode another horse. In England they have plenty of very bad-tempered horses, and some of the sires are absolutely savage. Mr. W. E. Deakin once went in to The Marquis, which came from England, a savage, and the horse soon had him down, and was proceeding to worry him when a flank attack by a lad with a pitchfork took the savage's attention off Mr. Deakin, and he got out of the box. Winterlake was shot by Mr. Blackler because unmanageable. Planter is a real savage; years ago (1873) he pulled a boy off his mount. Dunkeld squatted upon his buttocks, old-man kangaroo fashion, and pawed at Mr. Watson. For absolute savagery a horse called Cyclops, belonging to Mr. John Colbham, takes the cake. He killed one man and maimed two more."

October 27, 1906.—" A wild customer Wandin is on a race-course. He banged into the gate going on to the course. Charles Stuart cannot stay. Little Fig was 'not quite ready,' or perhaps the distance was too far. Fifeness seems to have lost his form. Czarovitch found the weight too much for him. Not long ago Mr. McDonald and Mr. James Scobie were very dangerous in all races. Now neither can win a race of any kind."

November 29, 1906.—" The New Zealand Cup this year dwindled down to a poor field of very ordinary horses. Mr. Stead had nothing worth running."

December 8, 1906.—" It may be that increased pace has brought with it a lack of soundness. The French horses, with one exception, Maintenon, were not good this year. The three-year-olds of 1906 were a middling lot."

Ibid.—" At the Traralyon Show the blood horses were not by any means what one would expect to meet with. There was nothing on the ground of quality to get all-round horses of the kind shippers for outside markets are in constant need of. The present sires are more likely to throw fast squabby weeds, for they represent neither size, bone, nor quality."

February 28, 1907.—" The old theory that racing improves the breed of horses has long since been exploded. Sprint races and light handicaps have turned the thoroughbred—once the finest saddle-horse in the world—into a leggy weed. It is now admitted in England that he is unfitted to carry a man to hounds. The thoroughbred is therefore unfitted to raise saddle-horses of sufficient stamina to withstand the severe test of a campaign."

March 17, 1907.—" The New South Wales bred two-year-olds are a very ordinary lot. Nothing seems to stand out. Boastful is a puzzle; she has disappointed time and again this autumn. Lady Diffidence, very much fancied, ran last. Dinlius is fast, but will not work and eat at the same time. Emir had to be galloped every day of his life or no boy could sit on him. Saraband is a glutton for work, but shows no pace."

May 11, 1907.—" Twenty starters for the Welter Handicap were such a poor lot that old Narelle was as good a favourite as anything. Alexis gave a deal of trouble at the post."

June 22, 1907.—" If horse-breeding is to occupy the important position it has done hitherto, it can be done only by exercising more judgment in breeding. Generally speaking, it is conducted in a haphazard manner. Mares are bred from, because they are on the place and not much use for work. The sire must be near by and not expensive; there is often not even a thought of selection. A very second-rate lot of two-years-olds did duty in the Minook Nursery. Grafton Belle, a light-waisted, leggy filly, lasted for half the journey."

July 6, 1907.—" A London paper makes the statement that it is now as difficult to obtain really good horses in England as it is to find the proverbial needle in the haystack."

July 20. 1907.—" The field at Epsom was looked upon as a moderate one. The race proved that Slieve Gallion lacked the necessary stamina. The Imperial Plate of 1,200 sovs. brought out a poor field, only seven moderate horses trying conclusions. At Lewes sport was of very poor class. Oakleigh II. is an erratic performer."

August 31, 1907.—" Of late years the thoroughbred horse has been regarded by British horse-breeders as not having sufficient strength and staying-power to serve as a sire for hunters. The product of grade sires on grade dams usually gave uncertain results. The American trotter is the product of a large infusion of the best thoroughbred blood. But, good as he is, I doubt if he would make a useful sire for raising remounts."

September 14, 1907.—" The sight of a horse hooded and blinkered, as Tangaroa was on Saturday, is quite common in England. The English race-horse is faster than the Australian. Where we have the advantage is in staying power, general soundness, and temper. The fear is that we get further away from the hardy old strains, and breed horses which will lose their reputation for hardiness and become more like the English horse of to-day. Pace will be increased at the expense of soundness and stamina. Race-horses are becoming more and more inbred, and, if this goes on much longer, there will probably be a collapse of the English thoroughbred. Horses are bigger and handsomer than ever they were, and some few of them are gifted with tremendous speed. But stayers are most difficult to find, and are decreasing numerically every year. There are far more roguish non-tryers than there ought to be, and far too many horses of delicate constitution who collapse prematurely if they have to undergo any extra strain. Class in race-horses means great speed. The wiry horse is almost unknown in these days, and one hears of far too many breakdowns."

September 21, 1907.—" In France, a brother to Flying Fox, named Pipistrello, attacked his groom in a paddock, inflicting injuries which resulted in the man's death. Mr. Allison says a real savage which he saw was Vatican.

This poor beast had his eyes put out to prevent him from seeing where to attack ; he was chained and roped in a most amazing manner. Other savages Mr. Allison knew in later days were the great Barcaldine, Beau Brummel, and Despair. 'Diamond Jubilee was a mad horse in his first season on the turf,' he writes. Beaudesert nearly killed his groom. George Frederick and Ladas are two other horses Mr. Allison mentions among savages. The English Two Thousand and St. Leger winner, The Marquis, was a villain of the deepest dye. Mr. W. E. Deakin resolved he would try and straighten The Marquis up, but the horse had him down in a twinkling, and was kneeling on his chest preparing for a worry when he was beaten off [this was previously mentioned]. Mr. S. Gardiner had a special box with two doors. The Marquis was let out into his yard through one while the groom slipped in the other and shut both doors. Winterlake, the imported horse who got Sandal and Isonomy, was supposed to have been shot by Mr. Blackler on account of his savage ways ; he worried his groom in Tasmania, and was shot while engaged in the performance. Gang Forward was tricky and not safe with strangers."

Ibid.—" It is a long time since such a bad lot have contested a suburban hurdle race. Darriwell was an abject failure at the stud. Mooltan's dam, Dilisk, has never produced a good one. Gibraltar was a failure at the stud."

September 28, 1907.—" The great majority of the expensive yearlings in England are often of little or no value for stud purposes. In the craving for fashion breeders ignore the question of suitability. In 1905 there were twenty-six four-figured yearlings, but only three of the number worthy of notice, and neither of these well-bred."

Then a considerable list of high-priced failures in Australia is given, and it is said there are numerous others. The writer cites an English writer who argues that by better understanding the principles of breeding it would be possible to produce more reliable yearlings.

November 9, 1907.—Dr. W. H. Lang, of Corowa, says it is quite a common thing to see half a dozen horses in one afternoon's steeplechasing with a tube in their throats.

November 23, 1907.—" New Zealand horses, taken all round, are nothing like what they were in the Musket period. . . . The sprinters in the Rosstown Plate were a weak lot. Perfection ran one of his worst races, and Paran died out softly."

December 7, 1907.—" Thirty-two horses were nominated for the Queensland Cup, but few, if any, of them can be classed as Cup horses, and it seems almost a certainty that the two miles will be run in comparatively slow time."

Ibid.—" Like so many Galopin horses, Grenelle is rather bad-tempered."

Ibid.—" For the Cambridgeshire, fifteen horses faced the starter, and the field was by no means a noteworthy one. . . . A very bad lot did duty in the Maiden Plate, in which three of the Pistols ran, but so far they have done nothing. Anyone looking at the photographs of racing in England must notice that often a third of the field are blinkered."

December 12, 1907.—" The Sir Tristram colt, Euroa, was fancied for the Queensland Cup, but behaved disappointingly, and the excuse was made for him that wet ground was not to his liking. He was backed again when the ground was dry, but he failed badly, and there is just a suspicion now that he is a bit of a rogue. The Grafton colt, Metograph, has been anything but a success, and the only other of the age who has any pretension of class, The Moulder, has for some time been developing soreness."

January 4, 1908.—" The last week of the year had plenty of racing of a sort, with the inevitable result of small fields and but a poor class of racing."

Ibid. — " A mile and a quarter was considered beyond Radiance, and so the sequel proved, as he shut up rather suddenly and finished absolutely last. . . . The remainder of the field were a poor lot. Limestone again ran very badly, and Ganymede and Destinist made a poor show. Over twenty horses contested the Brackley Handicap [England]; the majority of them of moderate class. Rambling Rector cost 2,000 guineas as a yearling, but has gone through the season without winning a single race."

January 25, 1908.—" Tangara would never have left the old country but for a wind infirmity. Antonio was no champion in England, but we do not seem to have many better horses out here. I heard certain prominent men say on Saturday how green and awkward the English race-horses are for any other purpose. One said that as hacks they are impossible. Mounted in the morning, they are at sixes and sevens, jumping all over the place. The young ones will fall in quietly enough behind the quiet old stager used to lead the team, but try to ride one of them by himself, and it is nearly as bad as driving a cow away from home."

February 1, 1908.—" A flighty Grafton filly gave a lot of trouble. Cooper could not keep Clemency straight. Waine Hill was very slow away from the barrier, where he was a bit bumptious. The horses running in the jumpers' flat races at present are a terribly bad lot."

February 8, 1908.—" With the exception of Mr. K. S. McLeod's two-year-old, there were no horses of much importance at Sandown Park on Saturday. I suppose it is no use thinking of Grenadier. He is a fine horse, but apparently cannot be trained. Unless Booran is at his best, the opposition will be very weak. Tulkeroo's chance is a muddling race. It is astonishing how often the Australian Cup is run to suit non-stayers. Melodeon is said to be a stayer, but I should doubt it. The imported Traquair is an excitable horse, and in England was very nasty. Of course he is a whistler. Badminton in public proved absolutely hopeless. A more confirmed pig of a horse has rarely been seen; he simply declines to make any sort of an effort."

February 29, 1908.—" Oreus looks a loose-made, sprawling sort of customer that will give his trainer a good deal of trouble. Wai-ila cut it very badly, and is a wild, soft-hearted customer. Kilbride is only a natty-looking little chap of the handicap class, too nervous in a race, and will not gallop when closely packed."

March 7, 1908.—" Unfortunately, our horses do not include many really good ones. It is very seldom such a bad lot of horses have run over hurdles as we saw on Saturday."

March 14, 1908.—" Queensland racing to-day is almost entirely in the hands of ' battlers,' who have mostly sprung from the ranks of stable dependents, and who play the game on the shrewdest scientific principles. Haakon is now reckoned one of the best of our three-year-olds, and it will be a bad look-out for the balance of our season's racing if it is to be estimated through him as a representative of the leading lights. It is a sad pity that some means cannot be discovered whereby the trend of Queensland racing may be turned in an upward direction. Commotion would not make his own pace, nor would he race to the right. Fryingpan was broken down. Malan again and again showed that he was very apt to run a bad race. At present we have a plethora of sprinters, but it is useless to ignore the fact that there was a lamentable lack of stayers at the recent autumn meetings. The horses capable of getting to the end of a solidly-run two miles' race could have been counted on the fingers of one hand. Nor is the deficiency purely local, as the same condition of affairs prevails throughout the Commonwealth."

March 28, 1908.—" The horses that run at Ballarat now are stones below the form of those which contested the Ballarat Double in the sixties and seventies. Fields were good, but very few of the horses running are above plating form. A very poor lot ran in the hurdle race. Yeovil was not in a racing humour, but in a sour mood, and hung out badly all the way."

May 2, 1908.—" Anyone who attended Randwick in the mornings could hear horses roaring in all directions. It is an infirmity that gets worse, never better. Slowly but surely the noise made by Mountain King increased ; he was not only beaten, but he was disgraced. Although there were so many horses running at Randwick, an Indian buyer in search of two or three good ones could find nothing to suit him. As a matter of fact, the best three-year-olds of the season knocked holes in their reputation. No really good two-year-old colt came to the fore at Randwick. There is no question that soon we will have any number of roarers about. There are plenty of them now, and they are on the increase."

May 9, 1908.—" It would be difficult to pick any year in the eighties or nineties in which there were not more good average horses available for export at the end of the season than there are now."

May 13, 1908.—" They had good racing in Adelaide on Saturday, but as a lot the horses were not in the same class as those which raced in the time of Pride of the Hills, Lockleys, Ace of Trumps, Impudence, and others."

May 23, 1908.—" Traquair is a beautiful thoroughbred, and was quite at the top of the tree in England until he became affected in the wind. Bill of Portland and Traquair were brilliant two-year-olds, who failed to race on because they became roarers."

May 30, 1908.—" The hurdle racers running were far from a good lot. At West Australia, Thor was regarded as the best of a bad lot for the May handicap. Strome proved to be the best of a bad lot in the Epsom Purse. Northwood, dying to nothing, only scraped home by a short half-head from Mahina."

July 11, 1908.—" I did not notice any taking horse in the Maiden Steeplechase. There certainly was nothing of the Great Western, Whernside, Hayseed, and Pirate kind. Delaware always does something he should not do."

August 1, 1908.—" Windlestrue had his toes in and his head up most of the way. Nushka got second, but it was a poor second. It is a pity the duffers could not have been barred. The tendency to-day is to produce sprinters, and not long-distance horses. A Tasmanian bred gelding by Cocos became a man-eater in Tasmania, and his short stud career was terminated about two years and a half ago."

August 8, 1901.—" In England, Dalgety has so far failed to win back a single penny of the £2,500 which he originally cost. His display was even more disappointing than any of his previous ones, for, although the race was palpably at his mercy, he resolutely refused to gallop. He is one of the most arrogant rogues in training."

August 15, 1908.—" As a three-year-old, Nigel was a squibby, greyhound-kind of gelding, who could win an occasional short-distance race in bad company. A hurdle racer has been aptly described as a horse too slow for the flat and not capable of jumping fences."

September 12, 1908.—" There were eleven starters for the Steeplechase, and a real bad lot they looked."

September 26, 1908.—" Races for bad horses are introduced to swell the fees and give the worst horse a chance of winning a race. Does the Australasian thoroughbred benefit by these weeds being kept on the Turf ? Would it not be better, instead of introducing handicaps for their benefit, to knock them on the head ? What, we should like to know, has a five-furlong race for third-class horses to do with the ' Sport of Kings ' ? The ' Sport of Kings ' and third-class sprinting do not seem to blend." Let me repeat here it is a libel on the great Kings to call racing " the Sport of Kings." And it is not an accurate quotation. " The Sport of Kings " was hunting—hunting lions, tigers, bears, and so on.

October 17, 1908.—" In Sydney last week there were three handicaps run at distances varying from a mile and a quarter and three-quarters, to which £1,400 was added by the club, and yet these races only produced twenty-

DETERIORATION, FROM *AUSTRALASIAN*

seven starters! The great majority cannot even stay a mile and a quarter. The list of brilliant horses up to a mile, and a mile and a half, which have failed through lack of stamina is pretty long. Hopscotch, a brilliant miler, started favourite, and was done with some distance from home."

October 24, 1908.—" The blood section [at Warnambool Show] was very poor. . . . There was no excuse for Pink 'Un; he failed because he could not see out a strongly-run mile and a half. Welcome Tryst was a disappointment. Bright Steel must have disappointed his owner. Knox can hardly be classed as a stayer. He failed as a stayer. He failed in the Melbourne Cup, and has never been successful in anything over a mile and a quarter."

October 31, 1908.—" Ripon was very dirty at the post, and swung round when the signal was given. Dhobi, like his dam, cannot get very far. Goldsign could not get a place in a bad field at Ballarat. . . . At the Port Adelaide Racing Club there were seventy-seven starters for the seven races, but the horses doing duty were for the most part moderates."

November 7, 1908.—" Sir Aylmer was backed for £32,000, and he made absolutely no show. Knox faded out before entering the straight, and this was about the end of Bobby. I am not enamoured of the two-year-olds we have seen so far. They seem a very ordinary lot. Another Melbourne Cup is over, and once more all the turf prophets have been floored. . . . Alawa did not stay. Peru's failure was even more surprising than that of Alawa. Verily, racing is a funny game."

December 5, 1908.—" The Stewards between November 21 and November 28 witnessed some wonderfully in-and-out performances. There were no good horses running at the different meetings, and bad horses do beat each other in the most perplexing manner."

December 12, 1908.—" In England probably there never have been so many of the big races won by outsiders. The King's colt Perrier was found to be of very little use. The American colt Norman II., who won the Two Thousand Guineas, is only moderate, and apparently the only good three-year-olds are Your Majesty and Llangwin.... The South Australians outside Lord Carlyon are badly off for first-class horses. And the horses running are not what they were in the days of Sir Thomas Elder, the Reids, Harts, Bowmans, Piles, Croziers, Rounsevells, etc."

January 9, 1909.—" I never remember seeing so many lame or sore horses to go to the post for a race before. Half the lot that started [at Randwick] could not reach out at all when they cantered. It was just a case of a number of indifferent horses beating and being beaten in turn. Lady Carbine has been a prolific breeder, but so far her stud record has hardly come up to expectations. Trentmoon could never be trained. Banksia's record at the stud has been poor."

January 16, 1909.—" Several of the best horses went wrong. There are but very few good class ones about. Cameron is a poor finisher. Mr. James Wilson, junr., was unlucky in buying the imported Ormenus. Of all the horses that have discredited Australia in England, Noctuiform bears away the palm. Charles Stuart was a good two-year-old, but he never was any good afterwards. Cranberry was doomed to fail. Oban and Survivor were a couple of frauds. Abercorn was a failure in England. Far better to breed from the best here than to keep on importing low-priced sires that English breeders will not have at any price—horses that England has no use for."

February 27, 1909.—The South Australian handicapper was at Caulfield, naturally taking stock of the jumpers. I think he must have come to the conclusion that they were a pretty bad lot."

March 20, 1909.—*Tasmanian Turf*: " So far there do not seem to have been any young horses of promise among the locally bred ones making a first appearance on a racecourse."

March 27, 1909.—At the autumn campaign in South Australia there are not likely to be many of first-class running. There are very few good horses about just now. We breed three times as many yearlings as we did twenty-five years ago, but for some reason or other we seem to develop few race-horses."

April 10, 1909.—" Large, strongly-built animals, which are often spoken of as possessing great constitution, are frequently tainted with constitutional hereditary disease. . . . In the way of racing the want of good horses will be felt. No fewer than sixty of the seventy-five horses entered came out and raced, but they were a poor lot. Wolseley was favourite, but he is one of the poorest stayers racing. Player, unfortunately, has a bee in his bonnet, and you never can tell how he will conduct himself in a race."

May 1, 1909.—" No horses of any consequence ran at Sandown Park. Akim Foo, wearing blinkers, was very bad. After a somewhat long delay at the post, caused by the fractiousness of several of the runners, a good start was effected."

May 8, 1909.—" With three opponents on Tuesday of anything but high class, the Whirlpool gave a most disappointing display."

Ibid.—" Lord Strathmore made a sorry showing over the sticks. Eleven went to the post. The class, however, was very poor. Our second division horses are moderate indeed. The result showed that the local horses are very poor. There was a large field for the Maiden Plate, but they were such a bad lot that nearly 4 to 1 was laid on Doughty."

May 29, 1909.—" A letter [from Calcutta] from a friend of James Watson refers to the difficulty which Indian owners are now finding in obtaining their requirements in Australia, owing to the dearth of horses of the stamp required. The leading Indian sporting weekly, the *Asian*, says that Australia is in danger of being entirely cut out. The hurdle racers in the Grand Annual must have been a poor lot. The Victory became fractious in his box and split his pastern; he had to be destroyed. The ill-mannered

Sportsman went through and over two hurdles. There were thirteen runners for the Two-Year-Old Handicap, made up of second-raters."

June 5, 1909.—" That mulish brute, Brian Boru, was allowed to go to the post again. After backing into the barrier and breaking it, he was left, and whipped round and stood stock still."

June 19, 1909.—" The Irish correspondent of the *Sportsman* wrote that the poor quality emphasized the nakedness of the land as to jumpers, except Natty Maher. The others could scarcely be deemed worthy of figure."

June 26, 1909.—" The two-year-olds were a poor lot. Lord Derby had no chance, and Mutilator did not run as expected. Seddon faded out, and I expect it will not be long before the handsome fraud is gelded. Woorooma seems to be as great a rogue as Seddon. Jimmy Barbour met his death. Tracker has a habit of pulling."

July 6, 1909.—" The horses likely to run in the Grand National Hurdle Race appear to be a commonplace lot. There will be a large field of very indifferent horses stripped for the big hurdle race. A number of Grand National horses were out in the jumpers' flat race, but the majority of them shaped indifferently. Good stayers are not numerous in the old world. The two-year-olds running at this time of the year are a very shy lot. The Anniversary Handicap only brought out five runners. They were a poor lot. For the son of Cyllene a brilliant future was predicted, but he failed to win another race afterwards."

July 24, 1909.—" Last week the Committee agreed to give the treble handicap idea a trial. This seems very like a confession of weakness. Horses not good enough to run in the second divsion of a sprint handicap should not be encouraged. . . . The horse's head was generally pointing to the middle of the course and he ran a poor race. Finally he got Burn out of the saddle. Sergeant Brue ran one of his very bad races, and Sweet Bird is a

DETERIORATION, FROM *AUSTRALASIAN*

long time striking another patch of form. Trelo Vouni, who shot G. Lambert over his head before the start, was one of the leaders at the home turn, and was beaten fully 100 yards at the finish."

August 7, 1909.—Vaporise was heavily backed, but made a poor showing; he appears to be badly touched in the wind. The favourite, Oboe, was beaten out of her place."

August 14, 1909.—" In the class of thoroughbred stallions (light horses), the three- and under four-year-old stallions were a poor lot. Such thoroughbreds as were offered last week were mostly of the stallion sire class, and even buyers for this sort would have none of the weedy undersized animals which comprised some four-fifths of the stock offered. Over fifty trotting stallions were offered, and there was a melancholy procession of very cheap and nasty animals past the auctioneer's box. Hardly any horses with free-gaited trotting action were presented, and every horseman who does not aspire to win races on the trotting track is about sick of the sight of hobbling paces. There were a number of very young horses offered, and, generally speaking, the quality was below that presented last year."

August 21, 1909.—" No fewer than 120 horses took part in the A.R.C. Grand National Meeting, and there were 114 starters for seven events on Saturday. The dozen who did duty for the Grand National Steeplechase on Saturday were a poor lot. Concave appeared to have a decided chance, but was not started, so I suppose has not picked up his form. I wonder what is the matter with Paraloch. He was tailed off all the way. Sinderby was backed on the strength of a good gallop, but he ran with his head in the air; apparently he has no taste for racing. Jolaire was very nasty at the post, and finally he refused to leave until the others had gone a furlong. Apparently Siege Moi does not stay. Finnaseur, a great performer, was a very nervous horse, and during one of his displays of temper in his box he broke a pastern and sustained other injuries, from which he subsequently died. Curtain Lecture failed to stand training. He is a splendidly bred horse. Mr. Tom Ivory, another of the old-time racing men, is gone. He had horses right up to the middle of the eighties. Horses had to work in those days."

September 11, 1909.—" There are a number of supposed non-stayers among the acceptors, and, as for the Derby, I think I can pick out some that must have been left in by mistake. Are the Adelaide horses any good this year? It is hard to judge on the racing I saw, but old Waipuna carried nine stone three pounds and made mincemeat of the lot opposed to him in the Glenelg Handicap. Tarpon won the steeplechase, but apparently he had very little to beat. I am afraid the field was a very poor one. So far nothing stands out against the two-year-olds this year. Runners were hardly up to the average."

October 2, 1909.—" King o' Scots beat a poor field in the Carbine Hurdles. A poor lot of jumpers contested the Jaurdi Hurdles on the second day, and a very moderate performer in Double Eagle won. Monobel failed to win. Several trainers do not think the horses here are a good lot. Two have told me that their own teams are, with one or two exceptions, bad. Probably there are any number of smart sprinters about, but very few good distance horses."

October 16, 1909.—" The Tolo Welter is a poor sort of race, but suits owners of second-class horses. The field will not be a remarkably strong one as far as the quality of the competitors is concerned, but it will be a large one. It is to be hoped these 'plate and purse' horses will not last long enough to get in the lead of the good ones. The English horses after a couple of seasons or so cannot be depended upon to do their best; they become sick of racing, and either play up at the barrier or sulk after they leave the barrier."

October 22, 1909.—" Woorooma again gave a very poor display, stopped, and could not be persuaded to go on again. Osin, who ran so badly in a race at Williamstown, lately died out very softly. You would hardly expect a horse by Finland from Gossip to be a stayer. There are some very bad horses entered for the Perth Cup this year."

October 30, 1909.—" It has been said that the ' class ' of the horses entered for this year's Moonee Valley Cup surpassed that of any previous year. This may have been so, but the class of the starters certainly did not come up to the class of several of the early years."

November 6, 1909.—" A good many of the 1908 yearlings can go fast enough to win short distance races. Their weakness is want of stamina, and wind troubles are more common than they were. The horses which ran for the Derby on Saturday were not a credit to Australia. What a mean lot they would have looked alongside Darebin, Commotion, and Somnus, who were in the Derby of 1881 !"

December 4, 1909.—" Prætor had the reputation of being very faint-hearted, and was often filled up with whisky before a race."

December 18, 1909.—" Half the horses handicapped for the steeplechase were scratched, and the half-dozen left were so moderate that the ancient Earl of Castles was quite the pick. Goshen, as usual, showed pace, but he stopped to nothing. All the six hit hard at a 3 feet 11 inches fence opposite the stand the first time, and Bassanio was nearly down at it the second time. Yokohama and Hawkeye fell, while Bassanio jumped badly all through, and apparently he is not much good."

January 8, 1910.—" Although Australian mares, whose origin is obscure, have done so well as producers of winners, sires tracing to these mares have, generally speaking, been failures at the stud. The Barb was the Carbine of his time, but his stud achievements did not rank anywhere near his deeds on the race-course ; his name as the sire of winner appears but rarely. Cutty Sark was a great performer, but a moderate sire ; although a horse of great quality, he achieved little distinction as a sire."

January 15, 1910.—" Any old sort of horse or race will serve the purpose for which the majority of the crowd were at Mentone on Saturday. One horse is as good as another for a gamble. . . . The Kishengarh team are at present warm favourites. A good native team is always a bad one to tackle. I have been looking at this team's ponies, and they are certainly a superb collection of high-class Arabs."

January 22, 1910. Scobie was one of the finest yearlings ever seen in a sale-ring, but on the race-course he has been a great disappointment. Brasseur can gallop, but I suppose he and Noonday will die out towards the finish."

March 12, 1910.—" The absence of three of the star performers of the time, when we have a few good ones and a great many indifferent ones, made all the difference to the meeting. Take away Ripon, and the jumpers were a bad lot indeed. Does this mean bad riding or are some trainers putting razor-like toe-clips on their horses? Something appeared to happen to Sentorius soon after the start. Eye Glass, another fancied one, was constantly in trouble. There were only seven starters, and it was a poor field."

CHAPTER XVII

DETERIORATION, AS GATHERED FROM NEWSPAPERS GENERALLY

I NOW set out some extracts from various other newspapers, which have casually come to hand from all parts. They all tell the same tale of lamentable deterioration.

S. A. Register, August 14, 1902.—" The Report of the Horse and Mule-breeding Commission of the Government of India during 1900 and 1901, says of the Australian horse trade that the supply is decreasing and deteriorating. Not only has deterioration set in, but it is bound to increase rapidly, as many of the best mares have been sold."

Ibid., January, 1905.—" The number of lame, unsound, broken-kneed horses in Adelaide is yearly increasing, and it is said that a really sound animal will soon be a thing of the past."

Farm, Field, and Fireside, 1905.—" Roaring and whistling, and kindred diseases attack a horse more frequently than formerly, and one assumes that the increase has been commensurate with the increase or height and size of our light horses."

The Age, March 19, 1905.—" Anything we may do to check the deterioration which is taking place in the quality of our horses would be good sense and an Imperial service."

Truth, October 12, 1905.—" For some time past, whenever there have been ecstacies of enthusiasm about the prospects of an exciting race, something or other has happened to withdraw one or more of the competitors; when the sporting papers have been filled with lamentation over the collapse of a race there has often been an unexpectedly sensational issue."

Elder's Weekly Review, June 27, 1906.—" Good mares are very scarce, and we may be sure that a great many weeds and illgotten brutes will be used as dams."

Pastoralists' Review, January 15, 1907.—" For many years past the general breed of horses in Queensland has had the reputation of being the most inferior on the Australian continent, and it may be conceded that the ordinary best type of horse had for years suffered degeneration from neglect. It must also be admitted that on many occasions the class of sires used were not such as to keep the stamina for which Australian horses were notable in the earlier days of settlement. Before a Select Committee of both Houses of Parliament, evidence was given by many practical horse-breeders and buyers to the effect that our ordinary marketable horses were deficient in bone and muscle, entirely in accord with the almost unanimous evidence given before the Committee by buyers for Indian and other foreign markets."

Sydney Mail, July 24, 1907.—" The sport opened with a hurdle race, which ended in a farce. Only three ran, and one of these had little pretentions to winning form in the worst of company."

Ibid., August 28, 1907.—" The strapped-up racing-machine which, with few exception, is as useless for the road as the six-furlong galloping wasters."

Sporting Times, August 31, 1907.—" No one ever thought much of the three-year-old fillies this year, and they did not show to great advantage in the Yorkshire Oaks: they crawled for half the journey. It was cheering to see Lord Harewood's colours in the front, for he is one of those decreasing in number year by year who race for the pure love of the sport."

DETERIORATION. FROM NEWSPAPERS

Western Morning News, November 11, 1907.—" The Grand Sefton Steeplechase brought out fifteen runners. Glacis refused to run his race out, though by Carbine. Glassalt also passed on her unfortunate failing to her offspring Bonspiel II. . . . Polar Star only ran fairly, and may never prove to be greatly endowed with stamina. Slavetrader may be hardly good enough. Oakleigh II. ran badly in the Liverpool Cup. Keystone II. has given only disappointing displays. . . . Hanover Square seems hardly good enough. Shilfa is none too sound. . . . Laomedia is only a moderate mare, even if an Oaks second. . . . Whinbloom has done nothing during the season. . . . Burscough lacks class."

The Badminton Magazine, December, 1907.—" Marlborough, a hopeless failure as a flat-racer, equally useless at steeplechasing, was given to a brother officer, but took a dislike to military duties, and was as great a failure on parade as he had been on the race-course. His new owner thought to make him earn his living by pulling a dog-cart, but he ran backwards with it, and smashed both the trap and shop window. Three times his gallant owner put him at a jump, and three times did that useless brute gallop bang into the middle of it."

S. A. Register, December 17, 1907.—" The Hon. J. J. Duncan said that he had been associated with horsebreeding all his life, and that the breed had deteriorated of late years. Years ago, horses were bred that could gallop long distances with substantial weights on their backs. Now they breed weeds to carry only a boy over a few furlongs, and he attributed the result to the totalizator."

The Advertiser, March 2, 1908.—" The condition of the South Australian trade is not satisfactory, as suitable horses are hard to get, though the Indian Army Remount Department are offering £45 apiece for them. . . . At Flemington, Encambene got out of hand in the Corinthian Handicap, careering round the course and up and down the straight, and unseated his jockey, who is suffering from concussion."

Fry's Magazine, July 7, 1908.—" Three thousand six hundred guineas was paid for a chestnut colt by Persimmon out of Surprise-Me, which turned out a complete failure, never winning a single race. Rubio, the latest winner of the Grand National, was bought at public auction for fifteen guineas, the price of butcher's meat or a caravan nag."

S. A. Advertiser, July 3, 1908.—" An English farmer was unfavourably impressed by the way in which the mongrel element was allowed to manifest itself in Victoria among all classes of stock."

The Lone Hand, November 2, 1908.—" The early maturing horse, like the early maturing tree or human being, is not as tough as those of slower growth. A highly-strung animal like the thoroughbred horse is very easily overwrought by too much galloping. Only about one race-horse in three wins a race at all, while a tremendous percentage of those put into training never start in a race, so that their names never get into the calendar."

The Advertiser, October 18, 1909.—" Mr. Ritchie said racing produced horses of the kangaroo dog type, which were not a stamp useful on the road. If the legs and feet of the race-horses gave way on the turf, as they often did, it was not likely that horses of that type would be much use in ordinary work."

Elder's Weekly Review, December 27, 1909.—" Mr. Dutton's remarks upon the horses kept by the Clare farmers are curious and interesting. The breed of horses has dwindled very much, and, until that of strong, active hunters is again introduced, little improvement can be expected. The introduction of Suffolk Punch stallions would be of infinite use to the breeders of draught cattle, as they combine great strength with activity, and would help to banish out of the country that vile breed of heavy limbed black horses that have so long usurped the place of a more generally useful kind. The heavy black horse, commended by all English writers, as the English cart-horse, would have been far too large for the work of a Clare farm, and would eat too much to make the keep of him pay."

The Advertiser, January 8, 1910.—" That meeting confirmed me in the view that, if you take away the liquor facilities from patrons and the opportunity for gambling, it would be a very sorry, sick affair, lacking in variety, attractiveness, and the means of general diversion and enjoyment. A large amount of alcoholic drink was consumed at the races. I do not wonder that all those engaged in the liquor traffic are in favour of race-meetings."

Ibid., January 21, 1910.—" Mr. Brewer, on being asked, said racing in England was only carried on by the richer classes, and for this reason, therefore, it stood on a higher grade. . . . The English thoroughbred was a highly-strung animal, and was spoilt and pampered."

S. A. Register, February 1, 1910.—"' Horse-breeding has been neglected to a remarkable extent in recent years,' said a well-known Burra grazier a few days since. And, as a result, good animals can scarcely be secured for love or money. If some one does not start breeding soon, the horse will become an almost unobtainable quantity."

Garden and Field, February, 1910.—" The Collingrove pony stud, with some Shetland and Welsh mares thoroughbred, and a small infusion of Arab blood has been used, and the result has been a very handsome type of pony. The polo pony mare Rosemary, by Rosewater, won thirty-six firsts and champions. This mare came out in foal to the celebrated Mootrub. Mootrub is an Arab of the Seglawi Jedran strain from Nejd in Central Arabia, brought to England, where he won on all occasions shown, taking twenty-one first prizes. He is the sire of many prize-winners."

Elder's Weekly Review, February 9, 1910.—" To breed from, to get good upstanding hacks, get strong, clean-legged, active mares, cross them with an Arab to harden up the bone and give staying qualities, then re-cross again with the English thoroughbred."

Elder's Weekly Review, Ibid.—" Now, although this was not the first important importation of Eastern and foreign blood into England, I wish to emphasize the period and mark the influence of Arab blood. It is beyond argument that the introduction of Eastern blood has been a potent factor in improving the breed. I do not see the same grand class of upstanding hacks of twenty years ago. The Arab did not exactly found a new breed, but was merely a fresh infusion. No one undertakes long journeys in England by road in these days, and it is on this account that the hackney is now more for show than anything else. . . . In making a choice of a mare to breed from, I should always go for a moderately small one; they are generally endowed with a better constitution than very large ones."

S. A. Register, March 7, 1910.—" What with one thing and another, the sport provided during the two days at Caulfield and the four days at Flemington was just about as poor as has been witnessed for many years. The open events were correspondingly tame. There was a scarcity of good old horses running at the meeting."

The Advertiser, July 5, 1910.—" As to the Derby itself, of the fifteen starters only a third were deemed to possess any earthly chance."

The *Melbourne Herald* of November 16, 1910, cites Mr. F. W. Purches as a recognized authority on horse-breeding, who says that the race-horses of to-day are not better than they were twenty years ago; that there is a lack of hardness or a deficiency in quality. They are speedier, but they lack a valuable quality. The St. Simon blood, he says, has a highly strung nervous system and a shiftiness of nature, and lacks honesty. The English thoroughbred of to-day may be compared to a specialized hot-house plant.

CHAPTER XVIII

DETERIORATION ACCORDING TO SUNDRY BOOKS AND MAGAZINES

THIS chapter gives some extracts from various books and magazines, which go to prove and explain deterioration.

Nineteenth Century, March, 1894.—" Many of the thoroughbreds from Ireland are practically only the casts-off of the racing stables, too often purchased at a low price because they are useless and unsound."

Pearson's Magazine, October, 1905.—" There is difficulty in sketching a thoroughbred in a horsebox, owing to the vigorous protests of thoroughbreds against strangers in their quarters. Some people may admire those vigorous protests as English pluck, but it is very objectionable on a battle-field or on a scout."

Major Parry, in his " Sketch of the Suakim Campaign," 1885, states that the English horses were a seedy lot, and it would have been far better if they had had nothing but Arab horses. The mounted infantry, mounted on Arab horses, had much the best of it over the rough ground.

In " England's Horses for Peace and War," Mr. Vere de Vere Hunt says that, although fine specimens of the British horse are to be found, yet more unsoundness, weediness, and deformity than previously existed has marked our general horses of late years.

In a letter to the Royal Agricultural Society in November, 1863, Colonel Baker writes : " The deterioration of horses in Ireland is an evident and acknowledged fact. One cause is the dearth of good stallions and inability of the poor horse-breeder to make use of a superior sire, and the use of fashionable rather than sound and useful blood. The origin of the cause of complaint in the racing stables is the worn out, unsound, and diseased racer with false shapes, and past all patching and piecing, which is too frequently used as a sire. The majority of our general horses are the offspring of thoroughbred sires of which a very great majority are not chosen with regard to soundness, so that defects are transmitted to the offspring. The great bulk of Irish horse-breeders have effete, unsound, and highly objectionable outcasts of the racing stables. For one fine grown, sound, weight-carrying and long-running race-horse an abominably great number of unsound ' weedy ' half-milers, or four-furlong shadows, can be polled. A well-known sporting writer writes : ' Long races are not so popular as they used to be, owing to the difficulty of getting horses to stay the distance.' "

Mr. C. L. Goldman, in " With General French and the Cavalry in South Africa," says : " The proportion of unfit horses is astonishing. One might examine hundreds upon arrival without finding a single animal sound enough to go through a month's hard work. The class of horse required was a small, well-bred horse. A large number of those they had were soft, which gave in easily and had no heart."

Mr. John Gilmer Speed, in the *Century Magazine* of September, 1907, remarks that Lysonby, in America, started fifteen times, and won all except one of his races. His winnings aggregated $178,190 ; his shortest race was five-eighths of a mile, the longest two and a quarter miles, the aggregate length of all his races was twelve and a half miles, which represents the life work of the greatest horse of his day, probably the greatest of this generation, which facts do not inspire much faith in the

DETERIORATION ACCORDING TO BOOKS

value of the modern thoroughbred or in the improvement of the common stock.

In Sir Humphrey de Trafford's work, it is stated that on the discovery of gold in Australia, horses were bred anyhow, and by 1880 New South Wales was overstocked with underbred, useless horses. At the same time, the breed was contaminated by cart blood from England, and the whole spirit of the turf was changing, and the spirit of the gambler was abroad. " Many horses of to-day are weedy without bone and stamina, and, if not good for racing, are of no use for any other purpose. The ordinary breeder never has a chance of using the best horses. Then, too, the breeder is led away by the mere record of races won without reference to distance, weight, or horses defeated. There are some excellent Australians sent to India, but far fewer than there used to be. Australian horse-breeding is in danger also from a scarcity of suitable mares, which it might be possible to cure by mating selected mares with an Arab stallion. There is unanimity of evidence as to the past excellence of Australian light horses, and equal unanimity as to the rapidity of the decline in their value."

F. W. H. Crosland, in " Who Goes Racing ? " says that Lady Hasty showed how really bad are all the three-year-olds when she dismally failed in the Brighton Cup. The turf is really more venal and less scrupulous to-day than it has ever been in its previous history.

In the " By-Lanes and Downs of England," Sylvanus R. Bentley writes of a wretch called Voltri, a black, long-legged imposter that they managed to make a great favourite for the Derby. He describes another " brute " as high as a house with capped hocks and stringholt, called Big Tom of Lincoln. " ' The brute ' was a rig with the disposition of Satan."

Sir Walter Gilbey, in " Horse-breeding in England and India, and Army Horses Abroad," 1901, says : " The racer of the thirties was lighter than his ancestors, but he was far stouter and truer made than his modern descendant." Sir Walter cites Colonel Hallier's description of them as being generally handsome, but often shallow in girth and back rib, light in barrel, and from 70 to 80 per cent. leggy and deficient in bone. "Diseases of legs are more common among thoroughbred stock—*e.g.*, curb, bone spavin, are not infrequently shown. Few of this stock prove fit for British cavalry, and hardly one for horse or field artillery, but some are purchased for native cavalry."

In "The Penicuik Experiments," Professor Ewart, F.R.S., states that during the autumn (1898) he had had further evidence that the thoroughbred constitution is very delicate. "As a matter of fact, the English race-horse compared with the Arab is like the hothouse plant that only manages to hold its own when forced and nursed with unusual care, and after all, except for covering very short distances at a great speed, the majority of the hundreds annually bred are of comparatively little use. That there has been a falling off in the thoroughbred may be inferred from the smallness of the percentage of even tolerably successful horses out of the prodigious number bred at an enormous outlay. Reversion to the vigorous hardy horses of bygone days would be the salvation of the English race-horse."

In the *Pastoralists' Review* of July 15, 1907, a writer, describing a Maiden Hurdle race, says that he went down to Melbourne almost purposely to see La Carabine, so much in love was he with her breeding. He saw a miserable washy chestnut thing walking round the paddock, knuckling over on her hind fetlocks at almost every step. You could have knocked him down with a feather.

In "Riding Recollections and Turf Stories," Henry Custance says that "Mr. Smith had nearly forty horses in training, four of them good enough for anyone. The others could not win a saddle. Broomielaw, with his mouth wide open, was a savage but smart horse. He was not a success at the stud, as he transmitted his bad temper to most of his progeny. Beauharnais, a little black mare just under 14·2, was an extraordinary little animal, but had the most perfect action, like a greyhound bowling along." The author believes that, as

DETERIORATION ACCORDING TO BOOKS

a rule, horses fifty years ago were much better than they have been for the last twenty years.

Munsey's Magazine, November, 1904.—" Contests which test endurance no longer have a vogue. The thoroughbred has practically reached the limit of its development, and there is reason to fear that stamina and courage have been sacrificed to sprinting ability."

Ibid., April, 1905.—" The American Cavalry Horse," by Captain Wilmot E. Ellis, says that high-strung thoroughbreds demand care, and are inconsistent with the exigencies of active field work.

The Rapid Review, September, 1904.—" About 1,400 two-year-olds make their début on a race-course every season, but by the next year they have been so thoroughly tried, and the inefficients so carefully weeded out, that there remain only a dozen or so good enough to go to the post for the Derby."

In the *Badminton Magazine* for June, 1905, Mr. John Porter says horses transmit from generation to generation many of their eccentricities and tricks, and whatever the cause we do not now appear to have the same good honest sound horses we used to have.

The Badminton Magazine, October, 1905, gives a list of queer-tempered horses :

St. Maclou.	Kilglass.
Prince of Tyre.	Sweet Sounds.
Good Morning.	Von Strome.
Knight of Kars.	Persimmon.
Disguise II.	Diamond Jubilee.
Worcester.	Florizel II.
Best Man.	St. Symphorien.
Grave and Gay.	Tornado.
Pretty Polly.	Telesinus.
Ladas.	Robert the Devil.
Barcaldine.	Lowland Chief.
Sachem.	Fritz.
Black Arrow.	Bridge.
Vedas.	Cousie.
Magic.	Sandboy.

The Westminster Review, October, 1908.—" A breeder takes into account the number of type animals from which the selected animals have been bred. If an animal has bad ancestry, though to all appearances satisfactory, it is unlikely to breed true. If the animal is itself a bad example of good stock, then it may perpetuate the worst points of this stock."

Mr. J. G. Speed writes thus in the *Century Magazine* for November, 1908 : " The thoroughbred has been bred up till he is on an average more than 8 inches taller, and certainly also very much faster. But he has become a long-legged fellow, very nervous, lacking stamina, and notoriously unsound, so that he usually runs to the end of his career before he is four years old ; very frequently, indeed, before he is three. In continental countries much enterprise is shown in securing the best blood that may be had in other countries, not omitting the Desert of Arabia, whence comes the best and purest equine blood in all the world."

In an article on " Army Administration : Past and Present," in *Blackwood's Magazine* for September, 1909, Colonel G. K. Scott Moncrieff says : " In spite of the fact that we are a horse-loving nation, our horsemanship leaves much to be desired."

In an article on " The Cult of the Unfit," in the *Fortnightly Review* for August, 1909, E. B. Iwan-Miller writes : " It seems that every disease to which animals are liable is due to man's interference. The hardiest of races deteriorate when the stimulus to struggle is diminished by the slackening of resistance. The Italian colonists of Rome went down before the Visigoths. The Visigoths went out of training, and could offer no resistance to the Arabs, who themselves succumbed to their hardier co-religionists. . . . The heroism displayed in the struggle to avoid the workhouse as the asylum of old age has been as invaluable to the State as it has been for the foundation of individual character. So the pampering of thoroughbreds softens and deteriorates the breed."

DETERIORATION ACCORDING TO BOOKS

Writing in *Fry's Magazine* for October, 1909, Mr. A. S. Galtrey remarks that " Pellison as a three-year-old was very bad-tempered. His temper even became worse as a four-year-old ; indeed, he became unmanageable, and it was impossible to do anything with him. Merry Miser was so mad that she always ran away from the post, and was not seen again for long after. Vedas, who won the Two Thousand Guineas, was quiet enough in the stable, but out of doors he was a perfect devil."

According to *Perkins' Christmas Annual*, for 1910, it was once said of the yearlings by Vedette that they ought to be sold by the gross, so numerous were they, and, as a rule, so bad.

Fry's Magazine, September, 1910.—" Race-horses of to-day are nervous, highly-strung animals, and, even if they do not actually possess greater brain power than their ancestors, they seem at all events to be much more inclined to act in accordance with their own volition," which is a mode of saying that they are bad-tempered.

The Live Stock Journal, *p.* 71, 1911.—" Mr. Milne was very much struck with the number of badly-shaped stallions at the Thoroughbred Stallion Show in London this year, when he was judging, and he pitied many districts where such horses were sent for the want of anything better."

CHAPTER XIX

HORSE-RACING

I MUST say something about racing, because it is evidently that which, more than anything else, is ruining the thoroughbred, not that it is the racing itself which is doing so, but the breeding for the sake of gambling-racing, which is notoriously the fashion. It is all nonsense to say that racing is intended to improve the thoroughbred. It is not intended for anything of the sort. Originally, it may have been so, although I doubt even that; but in these days it is the last thing thought of. It is intended in these days to give some people amusement, and to give many people opportunities for gambling and plucking pigeons, and but for the gambling there would be little if any racing. Indeed, for the mere purpose of improving the breed of horses there would not be a single race run.

A lover of horses and of racing, who is a very estimable gentleman, a rider of racers, an owner of race-horses, often called in as an official on race-courses, once said to me that I would not find in the whole world in the same number of people the same amount of concentrated villainy that I would find on a race-course; in fact, a race-course illustrates a celebrated saying of the Tichborne claimant : " God made some men with brains and no money, and some men with money and no brains; and them as has money and no brains He made for them as has brains and no money."

As to the pretence that racing is in order to improve the breed, supposing that a horse-breeder in England bred horses really for that purpose, and that he had a stallion or two which would unmistakably do so in a high degree, but the foals of which would be rather too slow for modern gambling and racing; then suppose also that he had a stallion which would get foals which would be certain to win every race that they ran for during a year, although they would in all other respects be weeds —utter weeds and begetters of weeds—which horse would that breeder breed from? Why, from the latter! He would prefer a scrubber whose foals would win him half a million of money to a solid sire that would improve the general utility of his foals for all time. At least, nine hundred and ninety-nine thousand out of a million would do so.

The hollowness of the pretence that it was to improve the breed of horses would soon appear if betting were disallowed. If the reverend gentlemen who attack gambling for ethical reasons were to attack it also for worldly reasons, as tending to ruin horseflesh, they would sooner or later be successful. They need not drop their ethical arguments. They could throw them in, and I give them a few authorities that will put them on the track; and which, used with the eloquence and power which they can use, would be bound to have considerable effect. One of the most impudent of pretences is to pretend that horse-racing as now managed is "the Sport of Kings." It is enough to make the ghost of poor old Nimrod turn in his grave. He hunted lions, wild boars, at times probably tigers, and certainly panthers, besides other dangerous creatures, and to liken even by the use of a word Nimrod's hunting to the running of a set of sprinters with tubes in their throats and blinkers on their eyes is too utterly preposterous.

The nations of Asia, born horsemen who live on horses, certainly race. Their race-horses, however, are not racing "specialists," but their ordinary everyday horses, and they would scorn to race for half a mile; they run, too, for fifteen, or twenty, or thirty miles. I have no objection to racing in itself. I have no great objection even to betting, though I never made a bet on a horse-race. I know many excellent and worthy men who often bet. What I object to is the demoralizing scoundrelism which flocks to a race-course and degrades humanity; and, most of all, I object to the terrible temptation which betting on horses gives to boys, just entering into life, to their ruin.

They would not steal to bet, but they steal to pay the "debts of honour," which they recklessly incur. Debts of honour! incurred by putting faith in the low betting "spielers" of the race-course. Those boys would not bet except for the mobs and the excitement caused by mobs. I do not mean to say that boys would not be found to bet on other things occasionally, but they would not bet in the mad spirit and to the mad and ruinous extent that they do now, encouraged and urged on as they are by the wholesale public, racing and gambling excitement. It is a disgrace to our nation to permit it.

To post a name in respect of racing betting should be a felony; to threaten to post a name or threaten to expose or inform, or to do so against any person in respect of bets paid or unpaid should be a misdemeanour; and in any action brought against any person to recover money directly or indirectly incurred by, through, or in consequence of betting, the defendant should have judgment for the amount sued for. The evils springing from betting on horses are so terrible that they should be remorselessly put down, and, indeed, it would perhaps be desirable to extend such clauses to all gambling, but no gambling has the terrible consequences which racing betting has. I respectfully invite the Labour Party to look to this. It is, I firmly believe, of infinitely more importance to their party and to the nation to stop or check this evil than to get a few more voters on the roll of our Legislative Council.

What makes the betting so dangerous to youth is that racing debts are allowed to be termed " debts of honour " by society at large, and the gambler who does not pay his bet is liable to be " posted," which is social ostracism, so that a youth who has lost will steal to hide his shame if he cannot pay, whereas he would not as a rule steal in order to be able to bet. Posting might be an unobjectionable enough rule amongst men of the world and " spielers "—at all events, I have nothing to say about that—but it is cruel to our youth and discreditable to society, and injurious to the nation, to apply it to schoolboys and to young men just entering upon life.

The *Rapid Review*, December, 1904, says that the " increase of gambling is strongly marked among women as well as men." Of course, there would be gambling of some sort, even if there were no horse-racing, but that breeds it, nourishes it, vastly increases it, and keeps it going. But anyone who ever reads that *Review* can see how racing gambling increases gambling in other quarters and in respect of other sports, and demoralizes young Englishmen, and, according to the *Rapid Review*, young Englishwomen also.

Mr. Leopold de Rothschild, in the *Badminton Magazine*, January, 1905, says that racing is a business nowadays with one and all, and that the old-fashioned enthusiasm has vanished, except on rare occasions. Mr. Gollan says that the turf is crowded with people chiefly of the wrong kind, and that there are not excellent folks sufficient to stem the tide of the less desirable, and the present condition of the turf is " bad." He wants to know what the Jockey Club has done for the horse, and he sets forth twenty-four different things which require to be done, amongst which is the closing of the Course to all "runners, tick-tackers, bonnets, lumberers, tale-tellers, spielers, and other predatory wild fowl." He says that the modern breeding has developed a special animal all nerves, long legs, straight joints, and short back to work long limbs rapidly. He also affirms that the thoroughbred creature is useless for sireing steeplechasers, hunting, or cavalry horses; that racing is a gigantic money-making (or money-losing) business, and he quotes the *Daily News*, which declares that the turf is a gambling machine, run and controlled by gamblers.

The South Australian Register, January 30, 1905, says that racing is a business nowadays with all and one, and it gives the quotation which I have just made from the *Badminton*.

The Advertiser, August 23, 1906, says that many audacious attempts have lately been made to circumvent the proper conduct of racing, the latest instance happening to-day at Bendigo, an attempt being made to assist an indifferent jumper by tampering with the jumps during the night.

The Australasian in 1906 said that the high prices obtained—Doncaster, 14,000 guineas; Diamond Jubilee, 30,000 guineas; Galtee More and Ard Patrick each 20,000 guineas; Sceptre, £25,000—are accounted for in a measure by the increase of racing all over the world. A man breeds from a thoroughbred because he may draw a prize for racing—that is, for gambling. The stakes are as a rule nothing by comparison.

The same paper, October 27, 1906, affirms that, " With the totalizator denied and wagering upon a race-course prohibited, racing in Victoria with the breeding of thoroughbred stock that hinge upon it would receive a death blow." I do not remember, and it is not worth while looking back to see, whether that is written by a racing man or a non-racing man: it proves what I have said, that it is gambling alone which keeps racing lively.

In an introduction to a little book on the London Daily Press, published by the Religious Tract Society, it is stated that " Horse-racing, except as a vehicle for betting, is practically non-existent."

The Australasian, February 1, 1908, quotes the *Illustrated and Dramatic News* as saying that it takes about £500 a year to keep an average horse. Some trainers are paid three guineas a week for a horse, and there are entries, forfeits, travelling, stabling away from home, jockeys' fees, possibly share of a jockey's retainer, plating, owner's travelling and hotel bills, colours, trainers' incidental expenses, and all sorts of little items. Why, even the marines would not believe that those items and " all the other little items " were expended only to improve the thoroughbred!

From The Australasian, November 28, 1908.—" For some time past it has been freely rumoured that an ' electric spur ' has been used by boys, and that, although no actual proof has been secured, there is no doubt that it has been used on unregistered courses, and the writer had an opportunity of inspecting one. It is switched on or off at will from the wrist, and a horse would make an unnatural effort when stirred up with it at the end of a race. At one of the unregistered meetings recently a jockey was caught with one on him just prior to a race, while a youth who was disqualified for life is said to have used one, and to have got rid of it before the inquiry."

The Advertiser, December 31, 1908, mentions an accident which occurred during the running of the last race, which brought about the death of a jockey on whom was found an electric appliance. The stewards came to the conclusion that the trainer of the horse directed the use of the battery connected with the spurs, and they disqualified him for life for malpractice. Except for the sad death of the unfortunate jockey, no one would ever have known of the use of this disgraceful implement of cruelty.

The Rev. Canon Horsley in 1907 took the prophecies in the daily papers, and compared them with the results. One hundred and fifty-six races were forecasted, and in 98 of them six sporting papers which were selected failed to name a single winner. For these 156 races, the six chief sporting papers nominated 898 horses, and 777 of them were wrong. The *Sportsman* nominated 197 winners, of which 170 were wrong. The *Sporting Life* nominated 155 winners, and 139 were wrong. The *Licensed Victualler* nominated 122 winners; 104 were wrong. *Land and Water* nominated 149 winners; 131 were wrong. Total nominations 898, of which 777 were wrong. The Duke of Portland, in order to put the matter to a practical test, sent £7 14s. to thirteen sporting prophets. The result was they sent him 19 winners and 95 losers. Of these prophets, 4 out of 13 were only able to guess 1 winner to 35 losers. On another occasion, the Canon selected 19 papers, and found that there were 13 right guesses against 114 wrong ones.

The Advertiser, September 2, 1907, relates that a man, I think in England, had sent £10 for six telegrams advising him to back certain horses, but none of the " certainties " won, and Judge Bacon declared him legally entitled to get the money back.

The same paper, November 24, 1908, states that " the reported offer of a retainer of £2,000 a season to Frank Wootton, the thirteen-year-old jockey, illustrates the possibilities of money-making in the saddle. To-day there are at least four boys in the States, all well under twenty, whose earnings exceed £2,000 a year. There is a fine opportunity for a very great sermon on this."

On December 10, 1908, the same paper states that in the Legislative Assembly in Victoria, Mr. Perry (Minister of Agriculture) laid upon the table a report by the Chief Inspector of Stock upon the effect of short-distance races on horsebreeding. " Races under 6 furlongs for horses three years old and over must be regarded as injurious and detrimental to the horse-breeding industry of the State, as they encourage the racing of animals devoid of stamina and quality." No one ever doubted it.

Truth, of April 14, 1910, says : " There is something at once melancholy, grotesque, and instructive on hearing that a boy has been solemnly reprimanded by a body of stewards for the offence of winning a race. . . . It is announced that the price of Minoru for the Derby is ' only 100 to 7.' Nobody who knows anything about it attaches a particle of importance to these betting returns, which are all balderdash, as there is no genuine market on the Derby or any other future race. There is always an outburst of crazy cackle of this kind at the opening of the season, and last year the gullish herd were tragically misled by the extravagant rhapsodies about Perrier." Who are the " gullish herd " the writer refers to ? Are they not those who believe that racing improves horseflesh ?

In " Who goes Racing ?" F. W. H. Crosland says that his brother gave an analysis of the prophecies of the sporting editor of one of the daily papers, from which it appeared that, if anyone had put five shillings on each of his nominations, he would have lost £50 in a month. This reminds me that I checked the tips given by " sports " in the papers for Onkaparinga in 1909, and I found that nine were right and twenty-six wrong.

Mr. Crosland also says that " the only way to get rid of sprinting is to abolish horse-racing, which exists simply and solely in order that people may bet. The decadence which has overtaken horse-racing during the past few years is shown by the circumstance that the ' Sport of Kings ' is nowadays very largely the sport of Shadrach, Meshach, and Abednego."

It is and always was a libel to call racing " The Sport of Kings." That term originated in, and was until of late years, applied to hunting, which develops manly and noble qualities. To kill a lion with a spear or an elephant with a butcher's cleaver, or to stick a wild boar, is sport for Kings—sport like Nimrod loved; but to prick a horse with an electrical machine, or to dose him with poison, is scarcely king-like.

"Kosmos," writing in Melbourne on the "Ruin of the Turf," says that "to make all betting illegal will be to reform the turf off the face of the earth. English owners keep horses for the purpose of making money. Common sense, experience, and statistics all prove conclusively that without betting there would be no turf. Betting is essential to the existence of the turf. If owners cannot back their horses, they will not run them for the public amusement. It is the bookmakers who all over the country keep up the interest in racing."

In the "Blue Ribbon of the Turf," L. H. Curzon says that "many a time, as sportsmen know, the second horse is better than the horse which wins the race. Why, it has been asked, should the chief jockey have an income equal to that of an Archbishop, and far more than is received by a Prime Minister, or a General in the army?" The answer to that question is because the chief jockey knows how to play the gambling machine better than an inferior jockey.

Dr. Ramsay Smith, the Adelaide Coroner, held an inquest on April 20, 1910, on a jockey killed in a race at Morphettville a day or two previously, and he found that it was dangerous to start a large field from the 7-furlong post under present conditions. He shrewdly added that the element of danger might be ignored if there were anything to show that it gave a good horse a better chance of winning any race, but there is not. Certainly not, I add. Very often, the best horse is not intended to win a race.

The National Review, August, 1904.—" Not only are the toils of our soldiers in the tremendous defiles of Thibet forgotten in admiration for the paltry performances of childish cricketers, but the stupendous and fateful drama which is being enacted by the banks of the Yalu falls in interest before the question of the triumph of a French or English racehorse." It is the example set by racing that encourages the mad lust of sport in other cases to the damage of our youth and to the detriment of the nation.

From *The Badminton Magazine*, October, 1904, it appears that the merest trifle may change the whole result of a race—a stumble near home, a bump, the faintest error of calculation on the part of the jockey, the slight swerving of a beaten companion, a change of leg, some little thing which, however, involves huge consequences. Those are all accidents, but the writer might have added physics, electricity, or the pulling of a rein, or the scores of other secret swindles which are indulged in.

That these are many is well known. His Honour Mr. Commissioner Russell said in the Insolvent Court in Adelaide, a little while ago, that the evidence before him showed another of the dirty transactions connected with the Turf, one of numerous and unfortunate facts which surrounded association with the sport.

Life says that the race-track is directly the largest agent, and the most successful, in recruiting for the criminal class. It makes more moral wrecks than any other. To say racing is the cause of finer horses is like saying that the consumption of milk improves the breed of cows. The real race-track is gambling, and it increases the breed of the thoroughbred rascal—for of the many breeds of rascals your gambler is the most thorough. A few of the owners of race-horses are rich men of character. The most of them are men whose secret thorghts would make daylight shudder. They are coldly, mercilessly, unscrupulously " on the make." To gamble is the fundamental, the real object of the race-track. " Without gambling there would not be a race-track or a racing-stable in the country. The race-track is responsible for most of the downfalls among the class of young men on which our future depends."

The Register, of February 27, 1905, quotes the Rev. H. Worrall, of Hobart, who had said that Tattersall's was an octopus that put its tentacles around the Commonwealth, and sucked the life-blood out of tens of thousands of people. It had drunk the tears and blood of industry, commerce, justice, and manhood.

Also on another occasion an article stated that " amongst those who attend race-meetings are tricksters, welshers, tale-tellers, monkey trickers, Yankee sweaters, thimble-riggers three-card tricksters, tote-readers, tick-tackers, tote-prayers, enough to make one ashamed of human nature—villainy untold and almost unimaginable."

In passing sentence on a prisoner in Sydney, Mr. Justice Pring called " betting on horse-races one of the worst vices of the community, responsible for more crime than any other vice he knew. It was sapping the life of the community. Week after week, young men sacrificed themselves to pay so-called debts of honour."

The Australasian complains that " the presence of the ' penciller ' is undermining the genuineness of many amateur contests, and reducing them to the level of money-making speculators." That quotation shows how racing gambling is pervading other sports.

The Advertiser, of December 16, 1905, reports Judge Egleson as saying that the case was one of the most painful he had had to deal with ; the prisoner had been swept into a whirlpool of gambling, which was rapidly tending to become a national curse.

On February 7, 1906, Judge Murray, in passing sentence for embezzling, said that gambling was one of the curses of New South Wales. A young man, guilty of stealing £100 belonging to the Bank of Australia, stated that horse-racing was responsible for his ruin.

The Advertiser, of July 16, 1906, mentioned that a brutal murder had been witnessed on the Flemington race-course, a hideous, revolting outrage committed by gamblers.

From *The Advertiser*, of November 16, 1909 (Wellington, New Zealand) : " To-day, in sentencing a young man who committed several offences of embezzlement in order to back race-horses, Mr. Justice Chapman said many youths were exposed to great temptation through the presence of bookmakers in the community, and the sooner it returned to the former system of betting the better."

Mr. John Gilmour Speed, in the *Century Magazine*, September, 1907, affirms that without bookmaking horse-racing as now conducted could not exist, for it is conducted for the sake of gambling, and the horses are used merely as part of the gambling machinery. " The reporters tell of the great wagers won, and a great win is regarded as a greater achievement than breeding a staunch horse." That is a moderate way of putting it.

A writer (I have mislaid the reference) complains that the sporting men, wherever they have got control, have killed every vestige of sport. " The best specimens of the racehorse are nearly perfect in symmetry, but not particularly useful except as runners on the race-course, for which purpose only are they valuable."

Mr. F. W. H. Crosland, in his book, " Who goes Racing?" says that the Casino circles of Europe may be iniquitous gambling hells, but he defies the worst of them to attract in a thousand years a tithe of the brazen knaves that you can meet at an English race-meeting in a single day. There is something about racing which makes always and inevitably for unscrupulousness and dishonour.

In " The England of To-day," translated from Oliveira Martius, the author says " that everything in England, absolutely everything, is turned into sport."

In the " Blue Ribbon of the Turf," L. H. Curzon writes : " In order to guard against the slightest deception, a body of mounted police had orders to escort the winner back to the stand, a very proper precaution, but affording sad cause for reflection that the whole system of racing has become so foul as to necessitate it."

Sir Hiram Maxim, in an article on " The Fallacy of Gambling " (*Pearson's Magazine*, September, 1909), says that for ten years he has made a careful inquiry, and all the old players have admitted to him that on an average they have only won back about one-third of the money they have staked. He states that about five years ago a certain gentleman made an experiment for the purpose of ascertaining the percentage against the player, and followed it up during the whole of the racing season, and the result was a percentage of thirty-two in favour of the bookmakers, whose making a book is just as much a business as is stock-broking. At Monte Carlo we have the amazing fact that the players have to place no less than £72,000,000 in order to give the Bank its profits of £1,200,000 per annum, and Sir Hiram scoffs at the idea of any system to win at gambling as utterly hopeless.

Bishop Mercer of Tasmania said that Australians worshipped the chance of getting somebody else's money for nothing. Horse-racing had always been a shady sort of affair.

The Advertiser, of August 13, 1907, states that "at the annual meeting of the Owners and Trainers Association the President said that the professional punter was the great bane of the race-course: those were the scoundrels who bribed jockeys and caused nine-tenths of the mischief that brought disgrace to the turf. They could swindle the public out of thousands of pounds without risk, and nothing could be done to them."

At Northampton, on October 6, 1907, Mr. John Ward, M.P., said that £25,000,000 a year was squandered on racing studs, and the cost of keeping up one stud would almost provide a whole country with old age pensions; and, besides the money squandered in keeping studs, another £25,000,000 was wasted by foolish members of society in betting. It was an absolute disgrace, for racing was no earthly use, but a positive injury to a great majority of our people. Racing was neither sport nor amusement, but merely something catering to an unhealthy excitement which bred cheating, lying, and swindling.

In the "History of the Royal Buckhounds," Mr. J. P. Hore says that the original intention at Ascot was that each animal was to carry 12 stone. An Act of Parliament (13 George II., c. 19) directed that five-year-old horses should carry 10 stone, six-year-olds 11 stone, and seven-year-olds 12 stone. The owner of any horse carrying less weight to forfeit £200. This national race-meeting was instituted in 1711, chiefly as an exhibition of speed and stamina by the horses, and a display of jockeyship by the riders. Nothing there about improving the breed. Even then the Earl of Pembroke, a good judge of a horse, who liked racing, disliked the surroundings of a racecourse (1715).

CHAPTER XX

CONCLUSION

THE preceding pages afford overwhelming evidence of the deterioration of the thoroughbred, the urgent need for the infusion of new blood, and the undeniable claims of the Arab. Of late, the science of Eugenics has attracted universal attention. All breeders know that it is of paramount importance in the case of horses, but, notwithstanding the elaborate efforts to breed upon the " figure " and other systems, the results satisfy nobody. It is impossible to predict with any confidence what the product may be. Out of the thousands of yearlings foaled annually a very large proportion are worthless; the majority of those put into training can never pay for their keep, while of the remainder the percentage of those capable of staying more than a mile is infinitesimal. The most highly-priced yearlings often prove a complete failure on the race-course; on the other hand, we constantly hear that a big race has been won by the offspring of some cast-off mare. As at present carried on, breeding is a lottery, pure and simple. Apart from uncertainty in other respects, the same animal can rarely be relied upon to perform consistently. From time to time, a horse like Sir Bevys, or Signorinetta, upsets all calculations by winning the Derby, and never earns another winning bracket, although Signorinetta did manage to secure the Oaks also in a weak field. Examples of horses with a single meritorious performance are notorious. To this general unreliability there are, of course, a few exceptions every year. As a rule, three or four horses stand out by themselves, but their pre-eminence only tends to emphasize the inferiority of the rest. The classic events are confined to an insignificant number of possible competitors out of hundreds of entries. Thought, time, and money are wasted in the vain endeavour to secure an animal of the desired quality, and thus it will continue so long as breeders refuse to abandon their antiquated methods. In considering this, I put on one side the rearing of racehorses as an instrument of gambling, because the sole justification of the Turf is that it can improve the breed of horses, and in this I unhesitatingly maintain that it conspicuously fails to-day.

The great defects are want of stamina, excessive nervousness, and frequent vice. As to the last point, yearlings, perfectly quiet and docile in the home paddocks, frequently change their character altogether when they have been two or three weeks with a trainer. This is probably caused in many instances by the rough handling of stable-lads, and by bad treatment when running as two-year-olds. The "American seat" is in no slight degree responsible for much of the suffering inflicted. The moment a two-year-old, frightened by the crowd and unfamiliar scene, begins to swerve, the small boy crouching over its neck is powerless to keep it straight; the whip is at once brought into use, and the animal mercilessly flogged. That punishment is never forgotten. With riders of the stamp of George Fordham these troubles did not arise; his were the seat and the "hands" which the modern jockey should try to acquire. Further restrictions, too, upon the racing of two-year-olds are needed. Nothing is more calculated to develop roaring and constitutional weakness than to overstrain a young horse when it ought to be steadily building up its strength. A movement is on foot to abolish 4-furlong races. Whether the minimum distance be 4 or 5 furlongs is not really of serious consequence; it would be of greater benefit to prohibit the competition of two-year-olds with older horses in open handicaps, where it occasionally happens that the two-year-old is weighted considerably in excess of one of five or six towards the end of the season. The two-year-old may be as good or better at the weights, but the risk of ruining it by putting too heavy a burden on its back makes it extremely unwise to attempt to bring horses of different ages together by any capricious scale of weights. Under three years, no animal ought to be permitted to engage in any except weight-for-age races. The consequence of this immature and incessant racing is that a good stayer over a distance of ground becomes more and more difficult to find.

Where are the Army remounts to come from? The demand for horses generally has rapidly diminished since the incursion of the motor, and any revival is problematical. But a regular supply of horses of the right type for the Army is imperative. The British Government cannot ignore this. The encouragement now given to farmers to breed suitable animals is wholly inadequate, and the price offered far too low to tempt a man to incur the danger of being saddled with two "misfits" for one horse that he can sell at a profit. It would pay the Government to go to almost any expense to insure that the requirements of the Army would be properly met without being driven in a panic, whenever war breaks out, to purchase inferior animals at increased cost from the remotest corners of the earth. For the different purposes of the Army, horses of various stamps are wanted, but the same qualities are indispensable to each. Tractability, intelligence, docility,

CONCLUSION

endurance, and soundness of wind and limb are the chief requisites. This combination of qualities characterizes the Arab in a unique degree. No impartial person can, I am convinced, read the testimony which I have collected from ancient history, from men of life-long experience, and from the leading authorities in every continent, without realizing that we must again have recourse to the pure Arab blood if we mean to produce what the Army calls for, and to resuscitate the thoroughbred.

It is unnecessary for me to dwell here upon what others have said with greater force than I can command. Whatever the defects of this book may be, it will have achieved its object if it lead some of those who are sincerely anxious for the improvement of horse-breeding to look to the Arab.

P.S.—Since the above was written, my attention has been drawn to the following memorandum, by Colonel Barrow, reprinted in Colonel Meysey Thompson's recent valuable book on "The Horse," on the Arab horses used by the 19th Hussars which he commanded in the campaign for the relief of Khartoum : " They were stallions of 14 hands, between eight and nine years old, and were bought in Syria and Lower Egypt at about £18 per head. Out of 350 horses during nine months in a hard campaign only twelve died from disease. The distance marched, irrespective of reconnaissances, etc., was over 1,500 miles, and the weight carried averaged over 14 stone. The weather during the last four months was very trying ; food was limited, and, during the desert march, water was very scarce. When General Stewart's column made its general advance on Metammeh, the 155 horses the 19th had with them marched to the Nile without having received a drop of water for fifty-five hours, and having had only one pound of grain, while some fifteen or twenty had no water for seventy hours. At the end of the campaign, and after a week's rest, the animals were handed over to the 20th Hussars at Assouan in as good order as when they left Wady Halfa nine months previously." This entirely corroborates all that I had written, Colonel Barrow's opinion being entitled to the highest respect, for he was one of the chief organizers of mounted infantry.

www.ingramcontent.com/pod-product-compliance
Lightning Source LLC
Chambersburg PA
CBHW031355230426
43670CB00006B/550